WOMEN
MENTORING
WOMEN

WOMEN MENTORING WOMEN

STRATEGIES AND STORIES TO LIFT AS WE RISE

MICHELLE RENALDO FERGUSON

NEW DEGREE PRESS

WOMEN MENTORING WOMEN
Strategies and Stories to Lift as We Rise

ISBN   979-8-88504-126-3 *Paperback*
          979-8-88504-756-2 *Kindle Ebook*
          979-8-88504-235-2 *Ebook*

For:

Mike and Anna
Brian and Lea
Donny, Molly, and Rory
Casey and Sidney
With Love

All profits after publishing costs will be donated to
Management Leadership for Tomorrow

CONTENTS

A NOTE TO MY READERS

Confidentiality is crucial in mentoring relationships. This book contains stories from and interviews of real people. Unless a person agreed to share her name and other details, I have changed names and further non-essential information to maintain confidentiality.

The book focuses on women mentoring women, and I have defaulted to using feminine pronouns (she/her/hers) in most cases and have used gender-neutral pronouns (they/them/theirs) in others. When referring to an individual, I have used their preferred pronouns.

In the chapter on Diversity, Equity, and Inclusion and elsewhere, I have followed the guidance provided by the American Psychological Association's "Equity, Diversity, and Inclusion" language guidelines.

INTRODUCTION

"There's a special place in hell for women who don't help other women."

MADELEINE ALBRIGHT

"JSUDF (Jackson State University Development Foundation) appoints Guyna Johnson as board chairman," read the text I received on a summer Tuesday evening. I almost cried. I wanted to hear more about it and immediately sent a highly emoji'ed text to schedule a time to talk.

Guyna (Gee) is a senior director and analytical manager at S&P Global Ratings. She graduated from Jackson State University (JSU) and holds a law degree from The Ohio State University. She purchased a lakefront condo in a Chicago high-rise after receiving a big, long-pursued promotion, and most importantly (at least for this book), she has been a mentoring partner of mine since 2004. Our partnership was part of the first phase of a corporate-wide mentoring program—a program that was "mentee driven."

The unlikely part of the story isn't that we are still in contact almost twenty years later or she was in the program that matched us. The first phase of that program grew out of an ERG (employee resource group) focused on women. Fifty of the fifty-five mentees were women. However, even though the focus of the ERG and the mentoring program pilot was women, well over 50 percent of the mentors were men. Men weren't more mentoring-minded: it was just a whole lot more of them were in the potential pool of mentors based on their seniority. I was the unlikely partner because I was a woman. My mentee was likely a woman; it was far less likely Gee's partner was a woman. Gee's goal was a senior leadership role, and I held that kind of role.

Gee was not the only woman seeking a senior leadership role. Almost two decades later, the percentage of women in senior leadership roles has increased, but not by much. The number of Women CEOs broke three records in 2021; there are now forty-one (8.2 percent) women among the Fortune 500, two Black women are part of that group (I will not do that math), and Karen Lynch is the highest-ranking female Fortune 500 CEO with her company, CVS at number four. The percentage of women CEOs has grown from 1.6 percent in 2004. No Black female CEOs were on the list until 2009 when Ursula Burns was appointed CEO of Xerox. I'll provide more information in Chapter 4. Women have made progress leading companies, but not nearly enough.

The vast majority of leaders in most industries is still white men: white male leaders made up most of the "mentor pool" since long before I met Gee. Yet, the percentage of male mentors is decreasing. In the #MeToo era, male leaders (as many as 60 percent, based on research) are now "fearful" of mentoring women. Menttium is a Minneapolis-based pioneer and leader in corporate leadership programs. Their CEO, Lynn Sontag, shared, in 1991, almost all of their mentors in cross-company mentoring programs were men; it's now down to 30 percent. Until 2021, Menttium's programs focused on female mentees.

I searched online for "mentoring quotes" and found 75 percent of the quotes were from men (thank God for Oprah and Maya Angelou). I did the same for "famous mentoring partnerships." The results were slightly better for women. The icing on the cake was the pile of books on mentoring I had checked out from the New York Public Library. Men wrote all but one.

Leadership development experts say mentoring is a critical component for career advancement for both women and men. The guidance of a trusted advisor supports professional and personal growth. Studies indicate an increased need for mentoring in our post-COVID world as employees grapple with a sense of isolation. People desire "tethering" to people they trust. Mentoring can provide support in dealing with the work-life integration and other issues COVID-19 has raised.

The statistics are disheartening, so let's get back to the positive impacts of mentoring—building great relationships and learning. Gee and I remain partners and continue to learn. While well-intentioned, I made more than my share of "rookie" mistakes but was committed to learning and growing as a mentor and leader. In addition to learning by doing, I have the privilege of speaking to dozens of mentors every year. They share their mentoring best practices—one included an improv class, so stay tuned—with other mentors including me.

The evolution of the serial mentors, mainly when it came to their motivation, was fascinating! The rookies' impetuses were usually something like "I want to pay it forward," "I had a great mentor," or "I want to share what I've learned." The veteran's response was far more compelling; "I learned a lot from my mentee, and I want to continue learning and growing." Mic drop!

In the very best mentoring relationships, both partners grow and learn. What would happen if we focused on mutual learning rather than just the mentee's professional growth? Could mentoring become a leadership development tool for mentors and their organizations? I think it can be, and I'll explore that in the "Selfish Mentoring" chapter.

I was in a meeting with a woman I've worked with over the past year, and after she relayed some of her challenges, I thought, "She needs a great mentor." I was not the right mentor for her; she needed guidance on work-life issues, and it was not an area of strength for me. Many of the mentoring-minded women I knew were close to mentoring burnout. We needed more women swimming in the mentoring pool. I sought to find a first-time mentor to support her.

As for me, I'm a self-proclaimed "serial mentor." I partici-pated in an exercise with a cohort of women I've bonded with over the last two years. The facilitator asked us to write words to describe each other. When it came to my turn, the most common word was "connector." This book connects my mentoring obsession, the stories of the people in my network, my passion for the advancement of women, and my drive for lifetime learning. I want to share all that with you.

My sincere wish is your mentoring experiences are as rewarding as mine has been. I've included stories to inspire and amuse you. My goal is to help you maximize your mentoring experiences to become a stronger leader.

Mentoring relationships should be mentee driven. A mentor can provide guidance, but the mentee needs to do much of the actual work. I will close this introduc-tion with the next chapter of the story (for now) about my mentee, Gee. A month after the initial text arrived, another message for JSU's Annual Day of Giving popped up on my phone. As board chairman, Gee had set a lofty financial goal for herself and the overall effort. I was hon-ored to help her achieve her goal. Supporting each other is what *Women Mentoring Women* is all about.

PART 1

ALL ABOUT MENTORING

CHAPTER 1

MENTORING 101

Mentor: an experienced and trusted advisor.

Mentoring has been around for a while—since 700 BCE reportedly. In Homer's epic poem, *The Odyssey,* Mentor was a friend of Odysseus. When Odysseus left to fight in the Trojan War, he entrusted Mentor with the care of his son, Telemachus. Not surprisingly, the first noted mentor and mentee were both men.

Traditionally, a mentoring relationship is between an older person and a younger, less experienced partner. Still, other types of mentoring, such as peer and reverse mentoring, are also effective (more on that later in the chapter). Who comes to mind when you think of a mentor? Steve Jobs? Oprah? Yoda?

Art of Mentoring's website defines mentor (noun) as an experienced and trusted advisor, and mentoring (verb) is to advise and train someone. But what exactly is mentoring? The definition is simple enough, but the full understanding and practice involves much more.

I'll share a story of my first experience as a mentor.

"I have a problem!" was the message on my voicemail from my mentee who graduated from high school two months earlier.

I just landed at Newark Liberty Airport on a Friday night. My flight from Boston was delayed multiple times due to thunderstorms in the northeast. It was one of those weeks: five cities in five days, and I was exhausted. But that message from a tearful eighteen-year-old got my attention.

Sidney recently graduated from a high school in the Bronx. I had proudly attended her graduation and hoped I deserved a little of the credit for it. She was my first mentee in a formal program my employer, the McGraw Hill Companies, sponsored. McGraw Hill is a leading education partner for millions of educators, learners, and professionals worldwide. The mentoring program grew out of McGraw Hill's commitment to education. The official program had ended, and technically, I was no longer her mentor.

Mentoring Takeaway
Mentoring relationships often outlive formal programs. That's a good thing!

I started imagining all of the problems an eighteen-year-old living in New York City could have and fretted over what impact it might have on her attending Penn State University in the fall. Sidney was the first in her family to go to college; she worked so hard for it. We had prepped for her college experience, including purchasing sheets for her dorm room and other supplies.

I took a breath, got into a calm mentor mindset (more on that later), and dialed her number. She picked up immediately.

There was no small talk. Sidney cried hysterically and finally blurted out, "I can't get to college." I didn't understand; Penn State accepted her. She graduated and worked out her financial aid. I reminded her of that. She responded, "No, I have no way to get there. I can't afford a plane or bus, and no one in my family drives."

I was a first-time mentor and tried to launch into problem-solving. The easy solution was to pay for her transportation. That was against the program rules, but our program technically ended when she graduated high school. I told her I needed a little time to think, and I would call her in the morning after some much-needed rest. Then I asked, "Remind me, what campus are you going to?"

"Beaver," she replied.

Beaver, Pennsylvania, is four hundred miles from the Bronx, thirty miles northwest of Pittsburgh. Translation: seven hours each way—if the traffic was okay. For the non-New Yorkers, you can sometimes walk across the George Washington Bridge faster than you can drive. Realistically, we were looking at eight to ten hours one way. Sidney seldom rode in a car, and we'd never spent more than two hours together.

I realized transportation was just part of the problem. This bright young woman had not been outside New York City since her family immigrated from the Dominican Republic when she was a child. She was making a massive move, physically, mentally, and emotionally. I thought about doing the physical part on her own. I recalled my first days away at college. My parents drove me to Indiana, a new place far from home, and most of the women in my dorm were like me. Sidney wouldn't have her family, and I suspected the other kids would be suburban/rural kids who drove to high school in an SUV—not on the subway.

Mentoring Takeaway
The apparent problem—transportation—may not be the real problem. You may need to probe to uncover the actual challenge.

Our mentoring program prohibited taking the students on private transportation. But we were done with the program, so I offered to pick her up in the Bronx—east of where I was living—and then make the four-hundred-mile trip west to Beaver. On the way, Sidney was a mix of excited and nervous. She frequently checked herself in the mirror and wanted to make an excellent first impression.

We arrived on campus to a sea of preppy-looking kids clad in khaki shorts, colorful shirts, and sundresses. Sidney wore jeans and a tank top. We unpacked the car and got her somewhat settled in her room. We met her roommate, who was, to our delight, also a city girl from upper Manhattan—someone who rode the subway and ate "dirty water dogs" from carts on the street. And she had traveled alone. She was quite a bit like Sidney, at least on the surface. After a busy day, we were all hungry and headed out to grab a bite before I made the trek home. At one point, the roommate referred to me as Sidney's "mother." I guess a safe assumption to her, even though I thought we looked nothing alike.

Sidney laughed and said, "She's not my mother."

"Well, who is she?" the roommate questioned.

Sidney explained the nature of our relationship, that I was her "mentor." Roomie's response was priceless: "I need to get me one of those."

It was a tearful goodbye, and I cried much of the way home. That trip somewhat prepared me for dropping my sons off at college. Four years later, I attended Sidney's graduation from Penn State University at the main campus, a mere two hundred miles away.

TYPES OF MENTORING:

The definition of mentoring sounds pretty straightforward, but there is no longer one kind of mentor. I'll provide some of the types of mentoring I've come across. This section may seem overly basic, but I'd ask you to consider whether you are doing more than one type of mentoring and whether you could benefit from sampling several options from this mentoring menu.

Mentoring relationships can be a combination of the following:

Formal: Partners/groups who participate in a program through an organization, school, community, or other groups. These relationships generally have some structure. My relationship with Sidney started as part of a formal program and then moved to our next type of mentoring.

Informal: Partners who connect independently, sometimes through a third party. It could be a one-to-one relationship or a group.

One-to-one: This is traditional mentoring like Mentor from the *Odyssey*. A more experienced person partners with a less seasoned mentee, focusing on the mentee's development. This partnership can be a formal or informal relationship. Think Maya Angelou mentoring Oprah, or Sidney and me.

Peer-to-peer: Individuals of approximately the same professional stature partner. This relationship is usually one-on-one but could be in a group. Again, it could be part of a formal program or informal. Schools and companies often have peer programs that partner new students or employees with a veteran who helps with integration and orientation. In this case, the "veteran" would mentor. There is also peer-to-peer mentoring which is pure mutual mentoring (both participants are mentors and mentees).

Group: In this arrangement, a group (sometimes called a circle or cohort) of mentees (generally six to twelve) are matched with a mentor or two to support the development of the mentees. In these groups, the mentees learn from the mentors and each other. These relationships tend to be formal due to the need for organization, especially if it's a large group.

For example, I participated in a cohort, G.R.O.W. (Gaining and Retaining Outstanding Women), through Rutgers Business School. Another mentor (with a different background) and I worked with eight mid-career women on topics they chose such as communication, networking, and executive presence. The mentees have the option to schedule one-on-one meetings with the mentors.

Reverse: The less experienced partner is the mentor to a more senior person in these partnerships. This structure allows executives living in the ivory tower to learn from others and often focuses on topics the mentee (the more senior person) is less than current on, such as technology, social media, or culture. This form of mentoring has been popular since the mid-90s and became trendy when former General Electric chairman Jack Welch implemented it. Reverse mentoring is usually one-on-one and can be formal or informal.

Here's a story of reverse mentoring in action.

I worked in the international group at McGraw Hill and assumed responsibility to turn around an unprofitable business in Latin America. While I technically worked in New York, I spent more than 50 percent of my time in Latin America, primarily Mexico City.

One of my biggest personal challenges was an unambiguous directive from the corporate security department and my boss that I was not to be anywhere other than my hotel room or the office unescorted for security reasons. I was more than accustomed to traveling outside the United States on my own and would spend nights and weekends walking to acclimate myself to the culture, people, and food.

As an American executive, I attempted to be as culturally sensitive as possible when traveling and dealing with colleagues, customers, and other business partners. When I met business colleagues, who were primarily men, in Latin America, they "leaned in," presumably for a friendly kiss on the cheek. I read books and studied websites, but I had a big question unanswered. "Who do I kiss?"

I asked my local mentee, now a newly minted cultural mentor. We were having breakfast at the restaurant in the Sheraton in Santa Fe, outside Mexico City, which was my home away from home. I ate my usual huevos rancheros and preferred tea from the selection I always had with me.

"What do you mean?" Pati asked. She was an elegant woman and a human resources leader. I explained I was confused when men, as almost everyone I was dealing with in Latin America was male, I had never met leaned in to kiss me on the cheek on our first meeting and all subsequent meetings.

"Everyone," she quickly responded.

I was confused. "Everyone? What about the angry customers? The partner who was less than truthful?"

Once more, she responded, "Everyone; it's what we do."

This conversation was well before COVID-19, and I've never been a germaphobe. I am a big hugger and often kiss people, including colleagues I know well. I thought back to our company's mandatory sexual harassment training and guidance to touch business associates from the elbow to hand only. I was mindful I was a woman, and they were all men.

I realized her guidance made my life easier in some ways; I didn't need to overthink kissing, and I often overthink. I just leaned in from that point on, and not once did I encounter a kiss that seemed inappropriate.

The lesson from this mentoring session was around understanding culture. There are often "book solutions," but on "people" issues, it's often better to ask a person—a cultural mentor, who need not be senior to you.

Mentoring Takeaway
Mentoring relationships can morph from one type to another or be a combination. In this case, I was mentoring Pati, but when I faced a challenge that she was more familiar with, she became my mentor—a combination of reverse mentoring and drive-by mentoring (more on that later).

Cross-Generational: This type involves pairing individuals from different generations with the goal of mutual growth, formally or informally. This form of mentoring has become more commonplace with five generations (Traditionalists, Baby Boomers, Generation X, Millennials, and Generation Z) in the labor pool.

"Ad hoc": This is not a standard term; a few of my mentoring buddies dubbed it "drive-by" mentoring. Perhaps situational mentoring is a better term. This type of mentoring is short-term; it could be just one session. The partners focus on one topic, often tactical, and could include issues like: is it time to shift jobs or careers, influencing and negotiating in a specific situation, or when to make an international move. My "kiss everyone" session was ad hoc mentoring. Organizations like the Small Business Administration offer ad hoc mentoring for entrepreneurs. Several author mentors supported me through writing this book.

Virtual: A specific type of mentoring in the past, but in our new normal, it's just mentoring. I mention it as it provides a perfect opportunity to expand your mentoring efforts. Are you still primarily mentoring locally, or have you used our new virtual world to partner with individuals outside your city, state, or country?

Speed: I think this is a misnomer. In these events, a mentee and mentor speak briefly, generally five to ten minutes. These meetings are really networking or answering a single question—not true mentoring. This can lead to another form of mentoring. I attended a session a few years ago and met a woman who was contemplating a career change. I suggested we have more conversations in which we went a bit more into detail, and I told her she might be at a sound stage in her career to pivot, which she did.

Self-Mentoring: In this form of mentoring, you draw on your skills and experiences to guide you. You assess what you need to learn and what skills to develop and serve as your own mentor.

"Self-mentoring, thus, is advisable for individuals who love the idea of growing, nurturing, and building their life without any outside influence."

DR. PREM JAGYASI, AUTHOR,
ENTREPRENEUR, AND PUBLIC SPEAKER.

Trier Bryant, co-founder & CEO of Just Work, spoke at a Chief event in November 2021. Chief is a private network designed for the most powerful women in executive leadership.

Here's Bryant's take on mixing and matching mentoring:

"The last part about leveraging your mentors is that I have also observed we see mentorship as very formal. Like will you be my mentor? Asking and making it very formal versus there are people I have come across professionally and personally who I don't ask them for permission to be my mentor. If I come to you more than twice for guidance, advice, perspective, or anything, you are my mentor, whether you know it or not. And that goes for people who have more experience than me or less experience than me. It doesn't matter. I have mentors who are the same age as some of the MLT students who keep me young and thriving.

If anyone asks, I'm twenty-five, and that gives me perspective on the things you know. I want to have perspective; I need to have the perspective to keep me on the edge of the work I do.

So, have I leveraged mentors? Yes. And I would probably say most of my mentors don't even know they play that role in my life. But I do the work to give them the space to show up in that way."

Trier Bryant takes full advantage of a "mentoring menu." She's an executive who both supports students and is mentored by them. She has a variety of mentors to suit her different needs. Some are long-term in nature, and some are ad hoc.

There is no excuse not to be involved with mentoring, regardless of your age, profession, or location.

Are there people you are unaware you are mentoring? You may be mentoring and not even know it, as Trier Bryant outlined.

In a Wharton study, Sun Microsystems reported mentors and mentees were six times more likely to be promoted. Mentoring is great for organizations too; they see increased engagement and productivity.

WHAT MENTORING IS NOT:

Now that we know a little about what mentoring is, let's explore what it's not.

- Mentoring is *not* management. A mentor is not responsible for managing the mentee daily on the performance of the mentee's job requirements. A manager is responsible for the performance of their team members. Managers may feel they are mentoring their teams; in fact, they are probably coaching their teams (that's part of the job of a leader). A mentor should be independent of her mentee in an organization. For example, you want to avoid mentoring those who report to you directly or indirectly.

- Mentoring is *not* sponsorship, although I think you should have both a sponsor and mentors. A sponsor is a person who must be in your organization—higher up the ladder, preferably two rungs or more. Your sponsor is the person who will look out for you when you are not in the room. This could be one of your bosses, superiors, or another senior person in your organization. If you are a financial manager, someone like a senior vice president of finance or the chief financial officer would be a terrific sponsor.

- Mentoring is *not* coaching or training. Coaching tended to be shorter-term and focused on a specific outcome, such as improving presentation skills, finding a job, or time management. Mentoring is relationship-driven and much broader in scope—overall development, perhaps focusing on a coaching area. In coaching, much of the effort is on the part of the coach; mentees should take the lead in their mentoring relationships. Another *big* difference—coaches generally charge for their services; mentors should not.

- Mentoring is *not* passive or casual. Mentoring is goal-driven and outcomes-focused. Think about Gee in the introduction. It requires a commitment from both parties and effort between mentoring sessions. An informal coffee chat to complain about your job while your partner sympathizes is not mentoring.

- Mentoring is *not* exclusive or a silver bullet. Most great mentors have a gaggle of mentees and love working with various partners. It's not realistic to expect a mentor to be 100 percent focused on her mentee outside mentoring meetings. On the flip side, a mentee may want to have several mentors—to support various growth areas and obtain multiple perspectives, and perhaps have a one-on-one relationship (or more) and participate in a circle or cohort. Most importantly, having a mentor does *not* mean you cannot be a mentor yourself.

- Mentoring is *not* one-size-fits-all. I've found there are advantages to having a few types of mentoring relationships, as there are different benefits in the various types of relationships. Perhaps you have one relationship in your organization, one with someone in your industry or community, and participate in a group arrangement.

I'll close this chapter with a story that illustrates mentoring missteps. Back in my mentoring rookie year, a younger woman in my company approached me about establishing a mentoring relationship. She gave a fabulous pitch, and I enthusiastically agreed to mentor her before doing *any* research on her. I won't be sharing her name or any details; my reasons will become apparent.

Let's call this mentee Mary. She showed up late for our first meeting—not an encouraging start. Before our meeting, I'd asked her to think about her career goals. After some chit-chat to establish rapport, we moved to discuss her professional goals. Over fifteen years later, her immediate response remains etched on my brain: "I want a two-level promotion because I need to make more money, and I want another baby. Do you think I should have a baby?"

At the time, I tended to jump right in with a solution, but Mary left me speechless. I wondered if she thought promotions just happened or, even worse, I could wave a magic wand and grant her a pay increase. I led Human Resources operations. I was more accustomed to goals that included more or different responsibilities in terms of career advancement.

I asked her to tell me more: what kind of role, additional responsibilities, anything. She told me she didn't want any more or different responsibilities—she just wanted more pay and more status. I asked if she thought her compensation was appropriate for her role and probed a bit more. I shared I could not be her sponsor (she didn't ask), as I knew little about her performance, potential, or ability. Mary added that she needed to leave her current role as she didn't see eye-to-eye with her boss and knew a less than fabulous performance review was on the way, leading to no raise. Mary again shared, "I really need to make more money."

We moved on. I suggested the decision to have children was a very personal matter and not a topic I was comfortable discussing, especially in our first conversation, as part of our first mentoring meeting. Work-life balance might be a better topic. I encourage work-life integration, and wish I was better. I was happy to have that conversation. At the time, I was raising my sons on my own and was pretty open about it. There were times I brought my sons to the office on weekends.

Any guesses what came next?

Tears. And let's say if I asked anything about what she shared next (detailed personal information), I violated ethics. I shared some guidelines for our formal mentoring program. We set a time for our next meeting, and I asked her to come back with more mentoring-appropriate goals. Again, guess what happened next.

Nothing! I never heard from her again.

I heard sometime later she had another healthy baby girl and resigned at the end of her maternity leave. I assumed this was a traditional mentoring relationship; Mary may have thought it was ad hoc. She achieved at least one of her goals. I learned to be clear about expectations in mentoring relationships—even ad hoc mentoring.

I've shared examples of some of my early mentoring experiences. Gee and I remain in touch; much of my development as a mentor has come from my relationship with her and other exceptional mentees. Sidney and I stayed in touch while in college; it was a positive experience for us. Mary and I were not a great match; I learned something from experience, and I hope she did too. I realized I could learn to be a better mentor. I'll share more of what I've learned in the coming pages.

CHAPTER 2

BEST PRACTICES

"A mentor allows you to see the hope inside yourself."

OPRAH WINFREY

You've just found the perfect mentee; you've scheduled your first meeting and can't wait to dive right in. You have so much to share with your new partner. You grab a coffee and are ready to click the Zoom link and...

Stop right there! This meeting is not just a coffee chat, and your mentee has entrusted you with her future. A little preparation and information can improve the experience for you and your partner. While I had formal mentor training—multiple times—and later facilitated mentor and mentee training, I'm still learning, and I've made many mistakes.

I co-founded a mentoring program at S&P Global-McGraw Hill. Initially, we focused on women just below the executive level, as that's where we were experiencing the highest turnover. It helps to have a partner who is a market research goddess. This group was leaving the company at a higher rate, so we started with them.

Soon after, we heard, "When can I join the mentoring program?" from employees at other levels. We tested a cohort with mentees deeper in the company. We tried expanding the program, made some course corrections, and welcomed more junior colleagues. One of our goals was inclusivity, and we expanded the levels of employees in the program to achieve that goal. Our most significant learning was that while the more senior mentees could articulate their goals and needs, our newest batch often needed help defining their goals. As one veteran mentor told me, "It's our role to help raise the goal-setting bar."

I thought I could effectively mentor almost anyone in the program, and I could do that—with some help.

By that time, I had been a senior vice president for fifteen years; my direct reports were vice presidents, and one was a senior vice president. While I sat in the "ivory tower," I thought I was still aware of my team members in the other ranks in the organization (I literally had team members who worked in the basement mailroom). I was wrong. And perhaps my fellow Implementation Team members (the people who implemented the mentoring program) knew and wanted to aid my learning.

On paper, I had whatever my new mentee was looking for in a mentor, and initially, that was our focus. I knew the business unit she worked in and somehow missed her title while doing my "due diligence." I guess that wasn't important to me.

My partner was one of the mentees in the most junior role in the program. Betty was an individual contributor and had held the same position for some time. She was a solid performer and wanted to figure out what was next in her career.

We launched our mentoring cohorts virtually, so the first time Betty and I met was by phone, even though we both worked in New York. Our program kick-off focused on getting to know each other as partners and quickly building trust. As was suggested at the launch, we scheduled our first few one-on-one meetings, which would be in person.

That first meeting was in my heavily wooded corner office on the forty-eighth floor of our headquarters building. The legal department shared the floor and wanted a "law firm" look. Everything about the space was formal: the decor, the people, the conversations. Betty arrived dressed a bit more casually than anyone on the floor. She wore slacks and a sweater; I and almost everyone else sported a suit. I had a small round table in my office, my preferred meeting spot for small meetings. A round table doesn't have a "head." If someone is sitting behind a desk, they presumably have the power. I thought I was eliminating the power dynamic.

Providing feedback at the end of each session is a great way to ensure both partners get what they need. I try to schedule a few minutes after each session to reflect and make notes. My mentee shared, "It was great," but I sensed some discomfort.

I realized other than assistants, who on that floor wore suits, employees of her level didn't meet with me one-on-one in that office. They did in an office in another location. This location was our corporate headquarters, and my floor housed mostly suit-wearing executives. I was out of my comfort zone regarding a different kind of visitor, which was good. Not so much for my mentee. She was not comfortable in "my" space—my office, my building. Our subsequent meetings were at the cafe in her building to create an environment better suited to mentoring.

Mentoring Takeaway
Physical location is a factor in mentoring. Consider how place impacts you and your partner.

That takeaway leads to our first mentoring tip. Here are some guidelines to maximize your mentoring experience.

- **Create a supportive environment**
The environment isn't just a physical thing. As the previous story depicts, the physical setting is essential. Start with limiting distractions; turn off notifications, close excess windows on your device. If possible, close the door. If you are meeting in person, think about whether the space adds an unwanted power dynamic. Are you in your office? Behind your desk? Even if it's Zoom, your physical space sends a message.

Encourage your partner to do the same wherever possible. Explore ways in which your physical space can support a goal. Take a walk-in person or do a virtual walking meeting, one of my favorite pastimes. I recall a fabulous story of a mentee whose goal was to get out of the office on time. Casey's, the mentor, solution: they met for coffee at 5:30 p.m. near the mentee's home, so there was no risk she'd return to the office.

Think about what time of day works best for you and your partner. I'm a morning person and prefer to do my mentoring sessions when I am fresh, and it is less likely my day has gotten away with me. That doesn't always work for my partners, so I need to be flexible. You'll want to have this conversation early in your relationship. I've seen too many partnerships fail because of poor time management.

In addition to the physical space, you must ensure psychological safety for your partner. Be open and judgment-free. Show you are concerned and engaged. Try to keep things positive or look at the positive side but be realistic.

- **Schedule in advance. Prepare an agenda.**
A good agenda will support accomplishing your goals in any meeting. It can be simple, and your mentee should send it to you in advance (I generally ask for it by the close of business the day before). The agenda can be pretty basic; something like this works:
  - Check-in/update/highs and lows
  - Status on goals
  - Deep dive on specific topic/goal

- Two-way feedback (more on that follows)
- Wrap up—confirm next meeting/action items

It's helpful to schedule out a few months in advance; if not, you could scramble each month to find a time that works. If you've agreed on what time and day works best for your partnership, you can schedule a recurring meeting. As a suggestion, have your mentee take the lead in scheduling; this helps her "own" her development. Be very mindful of canceling your sessions, especially at the last minute. That's another reason to be aware when you schedule your meetings; I don't think I've ever had to cancel a breakfast—in person or virtual—because someone scheduled an appointment at the same time.

- **Establish trust as quickly as possible.**
Trust is the foundation of solid mentoring partnerships. We know trust is essential in any healthy relationship; long-established trust can break in a flash. Let's try to avoid that.

Typically, trust builds gradually, but we need to accelerate the process in a mentoring relationship. You may have a short period (months) or a limited number of meetings, and you have work to do.

I've found a great place to start is to ask a question related to trust. Something like "Think of a person you trust completely. What does that look and feel like?" or "What does trust mean to you?" You can also ask your partner to share examples of trust in a relationship and violations of trust. Your partner's answers will illustrate what trust looks like to her.

Beyond that, be sure to honor your commitments. As mentors, we may want to overpromise; be realistic. Communicate openly, honestly, and consistently. Be vulnerable.

- **Keep it confidential**
Your mentoring conversations and what you may learn elsewhere must remain within the mentoring relationship unless both partners have agreed to share. For example, your mentee is exploring a new position; perhaps she's a marketing coordinator and hears about another department's newly created marketing role. She shares some concerns about making a move.

Be sure to ask permission before you share information, ask questions of others or make introductions. You know someone who has completed a similar move, so you offer to introduce your mentee to that person. Check with your mentee first! Or your mentee may want you to speak to her manager or a colleague to obtain feedback. Do not contact your mentee's coworkers unless she asks.

Of course, there is an exception to every rule, and there is no exception with mentoring "rules." You may have to break confidentiality if you unearth a risk of physical or other harm to your partner or if there are legal or other breaches. In almost twenty years and thousands of mentoring relationships (I oversaw thousands, I have not mentored thousands), I have seen this only once, and it happened to me.

It was a group mentoring program sponsored by another company and another industry. In one group session, a mentee revealed she feared physical harm from an estranged romantic partner who was a former colleague. Cathy claimed the man had allegedly hacked into her company's system. I suggested we take the conversation offline. I wasn't sure the entire group needed to be involved.

At the end of our one-on-one conversation, Cathy mentioned the Hard Rock Hotel; I responded, "I'm staying there; it's one of my favorites in Chicago!"

She replied, "I know, that's why I mentioned it."

My obvious response was, "How did you know? Did I say something about it?"

"No," she answered, "he (the estranged partner) did." It seemed odd that a total stranger would know or care about where I was staying.

As luck would have it, I was having dinner with a trusted colleague and peer mentor. Sarah Eubanks is a former managing director at Standard & Poor's. She had experience with women's initiatives and was one of my go-to people for anything involved with our women's initiative or anything mentoring- or leadership-related. I shared the story with her over cocktails. She asked a few questions (she's an outstanding mentor) and responded, "You know what you have to do."

I thought about it overnight and reported it to Human Resources the next day. The company was already aware, and an investigation was underway, but I felt I had done the right thing by everyone involved.

Mentoring Takeaway
It's great to have a mentor when you are a mentor; two heads are better than one. Having a sounding board can often help you and your mentees.

• **Get to know them personally**
Exploring non-resume information is part of building trust. Your "match" with your mentee (whether you found each other or had a third party—even AI paired you) probably focused on her professional development, but your mentee is a human being, not a machine.

One of the unique aspects of a mentoring relationship is exploring areas off-limits in a typical business relationship. Do you both like Thai food? Have crazy mothers? Love to travel? A passion for social justice? Speak French?

Focus on commonalities to start your relationship and explore your similarities. A word of caution here; while you want to get to know them personally, your conversations should focus on professional development.

I had a conversation about balancing personal and professional with a long-time mentee. Deirdre shared we "clicked" when we realized we both had a fascination with Jackie Kennedy Onassis. That shared interest led to a mentoring excursion to the Field Museum in Chicago to see Jackie's dresses (also see "have fun"). Deirdre added many of our family stories were similar despite geographic differences, cultures, and families' sizes. I'm the oldest of seven—you don't find that too often. We agreed upfront we would have coffee and a nibble at the end of the visit to cover mentoring topics.

Take the time to get more profound. Think about the iceberg graphic we've all seen. We often deal with what's above the surface. Attributes like hair and skin color, age, accent, height, and weight. Below the surface, we find things like life experiences, values, heritage, and beliefs. Start with what's above the surface but quickly move below the surface. You may discover that personal parts of your mentee impact her performance positively or negatively.

- **Set goals and define expectations**

A potential drawback of getting to know your partner personally is you may find a new friend and want to meet for dinner and chat. *Fight the temptation!* Your relationship is mentoring first.

If your mentee doesn't have goals for her career and growth and specifically for your partnership, make that job one. We want SMART goals—Specific, Measurable, Actionable, Realistic, and Time-bound. I would encourage you to raise the bar for your partner to set some stretch goals. *Put them in writing* and refer to them often.

- **Respect each other's time**

Start with showing up on time and ready to go all the time. Have your beverage of choice close by and your various "noise makers" disabled. Commit to being fully present for the entire mentoring session. If your energy is waning or your mindset is off (see "Mindset" chapter), do what you need to be fully present for your partner.

Remember your mentee's time is valuable too. You want adequate time for the meaty parts of your conversation and feedback. Add specific time blocks to the plan to prevent your check-in/update from taking over the meeting (it happens).

My friend and mentoring goddess Sue Stanek says, "Treat your mentoring partner like you would your most important customer." We all hate "those people" who live in firefighting mode and are constantly rescheduling. Firefighters seem to spend their lives dealing with sudden workplace emergencies. Don't be that person.

- **Freely and honestly give—and accept feedback.**
You may have been to mentor training, and you are committed to being a great mentor—and you've read this book—so how is it possible your mentee could have feedback for you? We know we should provide our mentees and colleagues with feedback, but we don't want to hurt their feelings. And we know we should welcome feedback from others, but it's so hard not to take it personally.

I had a coach who once told me, "feedback is a gift," which changed my view. Honest feedback is critical to the success of your mentoring relationship. If possible, make it part of every session. I've mentioned I am a morning person, and I love breakfast meetings. Well into our partnership, one of my mentees sheepishly told me the mornings were getting tough for her as a working mom. Easy enough to correct and a significant learning moment for me that what works for me may not work for my partner.

Be direct in your feedback and make it two-way. By making part of your agenda for each meeting, you will ensure it's timely. Make it as specific as possible. I once received second-hand feedback that a senior executive was impressed with my meeting participation. The input came months after the actual meeting. I asked my boss' manager for details (he was in the room) and he had none. I would have loved to do more of whatever I did, but I had no idea that that was!

• Listen

At some point in my career, the question "What traits do your favorite bosses share?" was raised. I quickly responded, "They ask great questions." Over time, I upped the ante on my answer and added, "...and they listen to the answer." I realized there needed to be something more as I thought about it. A prize-winning journalist asks excellent questions and has to listen during an interview.

Was there another piece to this puzzle, something that completed the trifecta? One day it dawned on me; the missing piece that distinguished a great leader from a great journalist was the great leader cares about the answer and the person who answers it.

My buddy, Marissa Fernandez, a certified professional coach and performance strategist, is among the best at this triple threat. It surprised me when she said she hadn't always been great at asking questions (I suspect she's always been extraordinary at caring), especially when mentoring.

In her early mentoring experiences, Marissa found herself "giving lots of advice" and "sharing wisdom." As she developed as a mentor and a leader, "I learned to ask more questions" and used a "mirror to allow others to find themselves" to "allow them to be their leader." Overall, Marissa spoke less.

Marissa, a former chief marketing officer, grew as a mentor and a leader because she established her mentoring relationships as learning opportunities for her mentee and herself. She has what psychologist, researcher, and *Mindset* author Carol S. Dweck calls a "growth" mindset. That mindset assumes you and others can grow and change (as opposed to a "fixed" mindset, which says qualities are innate and unchangeable). We'll explore mindset in Chapter Three.

Marissa's growth mindset allowed her to maximize her mentoring experiences for her very fortunate mentees and herself. A growth mindset is essential for both (or all in group situations) partners, but it's perhaps even more critical for mentors who may think they "know it all," or at least know a bit more than their mentee.

Marissa has taken the leap from chief marketing officer to executive coach, where she can turn her magic mirror on even more learners. As I thought about her mirror, my inner Disney princess said, "Mirror, mirror on the wall. Who is the fairest of them all?" What does your mentoring mirror reflect? Is the reflection a little fuzzy, and do I blame the dust on the mirror for the lack of clarity? We may think we have a mentoring magic wand to wave and expect mutual learning. That may work in fairy tales, but not so much in reality.

- **Maintain contact between formal sessions**
You can have great mentoring meetings; you set and stick to an agenda, focus on goals, exchange honest feedback, and still don't maximize your experience. Remember, mentoring is all about building relationships. When your communication is limited to one call or video meeting per month, it's hard to do that.

Start with what works best for your mentee. Does your partner prefer text, e-mail (business or personal), WhatsApp, or whatever? Are there times that are better for her? Does she want to be connected on social media, or is that off-limits? What's the best way to contact you if she needs you? That should not be through your assistant.

Both of you should set boundaries. I have established an evening shutdown routine, which includes putting my laptop to sleep and using my phone for only calls, audiobooks, and specific texts in the evening. After my shutdown, if an e-mail comes in from my mentee or anyone else, it will go unread for up to twelve hours. My mentees know that because I share that boundary.

Initially, I suggest at least weekly contact, a quick text of "How'd the meeting with your boss go?" or "What are you reading/watching?" I'll sometimes see an article or hear a TED talk or an interesting video relevant to our discussions and share that. Once your relationship is established, you can go longer between informal check-ins.

- **Have fun/be creative/mix it up**

We all have Zoom fatigue; one meeting seems to morph into the next, and I often think, "Who said that in which meeting?" Whatever cadence you've established with your partner, things will get boring if all you do is meet by phone/Zoom/in your office time after time. You might not be able to mix it up with your boss, but you can with your mentoring partner. And be creative. Have coffee together or Mexican food—even if it's virtual. Periodically meet in a different place or use a different mode. Are you meeting via Zoom? Do a call. Are you meeting in your office? Try a coffee shop.

My friend, Rose Lanard, is the queen of creativity in mentoring (and everything). Her mentee had a common struggle; she attended many meetings and prepared diligently for them. Despite her rigorous preparation, the mentee grappled with the inevitable curveballs that came her way, the questions that seemed to have nothing to with the topic of the meeting. One of my favorites was getting a question about the weight of a book (it was a big book) during a budget review.

Rose's solution: they attended an improvisation class together. In improv, you create and perform (usually music, comedy, or drama) spontaneously or without preparation. What fun! Again, explore whether the fun can support your mentee's development goals. Rose's guidance helped me realize I sometimes faced similar challenges, so I took an improvisation class; I was terrified and learned a lot.

One caution on having fun; keep your goals first and foremost. If you and your mentee share a love of Mexican food, have a serious conversation before the second margarita.

- **Share your network; make introductions.**
You may not have a more extensive network than your mentee, but you certainly have a different one. Don't limit your introductions to pure business; you may know someone who went to the same school or shares a personal interest. This approach goes two ways; ask your mentee for introductions.

I had a short-term mentoring partnership with a woman interested in pivoting from a finance role in publishing to a finance role in another industry. I connected her with a few people in finance (I was in publishing at the time). We lost contact, and she landed a new position at a luxury cosmetics company. I learned of her new job when I explored a role at her new company. I checked LinkedIn, and my former mentee had pivoted and worked at that target company. We met for a glass of wine, and my mentee offered to make an introduction connecting me to the hiring manager for the role I was pursuing. It's contagious!

- **Do things together**

Do things other than your mentoring meetings. Attend a conference or webinar together. One of my mentees, Katy, mentioned her boss was a massive fan of a particular business book. We agreed to read the book together and discuss it. We didn't love the book, but it was a view into her boss. Katy effectively used some of the author's buzzwords in her discussions with her boss. He told her he appreciated she wanted to learn more about his leadership style.

You may already incorporate some of these tips into your daily life. Some like "listen" are intuitive, others like "have fun" may not seem like an essential mentoring component. My goal in sharing them is to help you be more intentional and maximize your mentoring experience.

Next, we'll explore the mentoring mindset.

CHAPTER 3

MINDSET

mindset
/'mīndset/
noun
the established set of attitudes held by someone.

I used to think the world was divided into dog people vs. cat people, formal vs. casual, or sweet vs. salty. After reading *Mindset: The New Psychology of Success* by Carol S. Dweck, PhD, I realized the critical distinction is between people with a growth mindset and those with a fixed mindset. The most powerful advice in the book is "becoming is better than being."

In a fixed mindset, people believe their essential qualities—things like talent or intelligence—are fixed and not changeable. They tend to think all success stems from talent and intelligence; there's nothing they can do about it. Those with a growth mindset believe their essential qualities can be cultivated through their efforts. In Dweck's words, "A growth mindset is when students understand their abilities can be developed."

In 2018, the Program for International Student Assessment surveyed six hundred thousand fifteen-year-olds from seventy-eight countries and economies. Nearly two out of three students who participated demonstrated a growth mindset. More importantly, the students with a growth mindset (after controlling for socioeconomic and other differences) scored significantly higher on all subjects: 31.5 points in reading, 27 points in science, and 23 points in math (all on a 100-point scale, e.g., improved from 60 to 91.5) compared to the students who saw their intelligence as fixed.

But things aren't as simple as I initially thought; no one has a 100 percent growth mindset or a 100 percent fixed mindset. We're all a little bit of both. So, I asked myself, "How can mentoring help both parties shift to more of a growth mindset?" I suspect most mentees who seek a mentor—or two—have a growth mindset. They know another person can support their growth and learning. As Dweck suggests, these mentees believe they can cultivate these essentials through their efforts. Mentoring can move us up the growth mindset scale.

Patricia Romboletti is the author of *Bulletproof Your Career*, job search coach, and TEDx speaker. She's been hosting free weekly Zoom sessions since 2019. These sessions are open to all professionals and attract up to 950 "bullet proofers"—people who want to bulletproof their careers following Romboletti's methodology. Her premise is there are no permanent jobs anymore and professionals need to prepare for their next career transition at all times. This focus has been life-changing for me.

Romboletti's first three job search musts are 1) Mindset, 2) Mindset, and 3) *Mindset*. She goes as far as to suggest we set reminders on our phones to check our mindset and we should do nothing until our mindset is in the right place.

I asked myself if checking my mindset should be the first part of any mentoring session, and I could almost hear Pat on my shoulder shouting, "*Yes!*"

I did an Internet search on "mindset and mentoring." The first item that came up was from artofmentoring.com, which shared three parts of a mentoring mindset:

1. curiosity
2. respect for difference
3. humility

I have to admit I really love the first one! Speaking of curiosity, many years ago, at a job interview lunch, Terry McGraw, former chairman, president, and CEO of The McGraw Hill Companies, shared a great tip: to look for curiosity when interviewing potential job candidates and bosses. It's something that resonated with me, and I have incorporated it into interviews ever since!

Both partners need to have a beginner's mindset; it is significant for the mentee who needs to learn from the mentor. The mentor should be curious about the mentee; one size doesn't fit all. It's easy to think all mentees need the same guidance, especially when they seem alike on the surface. I mentored several Standard and Poor's (S&P)

analysts, and while they had the same fundamental role, their needs and personalities couldn't have been more different. I had introverts and extroverts, working moms and dads, and single women.

Mentors are in a unique position to "peel the onion," to get past the surface issues. For example, your mentee is anxious to find a new role. Her initial reasons may be something like "I want additional responsibility" or "I want to change industries." Explore what those answers mean. Get curious and go deeper. Curiosity leads to great questions. What do you need to know to support your mentee? What could additional responsibilities include? Is she prepared for those responsibilities? Does she need additional training?

Respect for difference is also essential. It's even more important to the mentor. While the mentor may have more experience or background in a different field, they must respect the mentee as a professional and human partner. Respect your mentee so mutual learning can occur. Often, mentors think a mentee should be a professional mirror image of themselves (same role or industry, not physical appearance) and believe they can best serve someone who has a similar background or experience. We all know and learn from people like us; we can learn much more from different people.

That's closely linked to humility; a mentor should see herself as a servant leader and realize the mentee has much to offer the mentor personally and professionally.

"It is unwise to be too sure of one's own wisdom."

It can be hard to be genuinely humble as the mentor in a mentoring relationship. Your partner has chosen you for your experience, leadership skills, and what you accomplished professionally or personally. You may have a better title, maybe a better car, and a more expensive home in a better neighborhood. Those things provide pride for you and could drift into arrogance or at least the appearance of hubris.

Worse, the trappings of the mentor's position and life can be an indicator of racial, economic, or educational privilege. I know that's the case for me. I've hosted several of my mentees for football weekends at the University of Notre Dame, my alma mater. I like doing it, so they must like doing it. It was almost a reflex reaction.

In at least one case, my mentoring partner and I shared a love for college football, and we planned a "football weekend." The only mentoring I provided before our trip was fashion oriented. In November, the "cute outfits," her phrase, she wore on game day in Mississippi were not weather-appropriate in northern Indiana. I wondered what my motives were in that outing. Was I showing off, in at least some way?

A goal for a mentor should be humility. In most cases, your partner is in a very different place than you are in every aspect of their life. You could invite your mentee to lunch at your exclusive club where they may not be comfortable and may not even know what to wear or own the appropriate clothing. Perhaps we should be a bit humbler and meet someplace more approachable, like a coffee shop.

Perhaps your mentoring partnerships can provide opportunities to explore how your privilege plays out in your daily conversations. Is it your weekend home in the Hamptons, front row seats at a game/show/concert, hanging with your prestigious college buddies, or the horrible wait at the Mercedes dealer, (which I've actually heard)? Could your focus on areas more relatable to your partner?

Can you take it one step further? Please share with your mentee you want to be a humble servant and value their feedback when you miss the mark. Be vulnerable enough to admit to your partner you know you are privileged and one of your goals in this partnership is to explore how that plays out and be more aware of your privilege.

I recall attending a party with a business school classmate. It was an afternoon event in lower Manhattan, and the attendees were the kinds of people who hosted fundraising events for "people who can donate at least one million dollars." It was one of those legendary New York City "no shoe parties." I was wearing a nice pair of boots, left at the door...and mismatched athletic socks. Everyone else was in colorful designer socks meant to be seen. I missed the sock memo; I wasn't part of the "shoeless" club.

The sock situation made me think about what other memos I miss in my mentoring and other relationships. When have I made someone feel out of place because of their figurative socks? This "out of place" feeling often ties into physical space, which I've discussed in Chapter 2. I found this when conducting mentoring meetings in my office; I was in the power (non-humble) position behind my desk. A shift in location to a neutral cafeteria allowed me to be humbler. It can be as basic as scheduling your mentoring meetings yourself—even if you have an assistant who usually manages your diary.

For all three aspects of mentoring mindset—curiosity, respect for difference, and humility—it's not just about you. It never is with mentoring. You may have developed those qualities, but how do they appear to your partner? For curiosity, do you ask questions or make comments based on what your mentee has said to show you are genuinely curious. With respecting differences, do you acknowledge your differences and celebrate them? This acknowledgment can be as simple as discussing holidays that your mentee celebrates, and you don't. Combining the first two characteristics, explore how your different backgrounds brought you to today and how that impacts your actions and decisions. Humility is hard, especially when you have been tapped on the shoulder because your mentee perceived you as more knowledgeable, experienced, or just more senior. You can show humility by acknowledging you don't have all the answers.

In a *Harvard Business Review* article, "How Age and Gender Affect Self-Improvement," the authors examined seven thousand self-assessments and focused on questions that measured "proving" versus "improving" orientation. The study may be biased as all respondents identified interest in personal development. The study found women were more likely to have a "proving" mindset, but fortunately, women shift to an "improving" mindset as they age. By their early sixties, women are more likely to have an "improving" mindset than their male peers. Women may be socialized to be "proving," but women—and men—can shift from the proving, or fixed, mindset to improving. Mentoring and mentors can aid and accelerate that transformation.

Art of Mentoring is an Australian-based business operating in over twenty-six countries globally. They have offered programs, consulting, and guidance on all things mentoring since 1997. They have an interesting logo that includes geese for a reason. "The geese on the Art of Mentoring logo represent the mentor/mentee relationship in the natural world. The geese at the front of the flock improve the aerodynamics to make it easier for the followers to fly. Geese at the back honk to encourage front geese to keep pushing forward. They are constantly shifting position, meaning the 'mentor' could be leading from behind or in front. Sometimes just flying alongside."

I've been one of those geese. I was in the middle of the flock for the first half of my career. I was open to learning new things, but in a somewhat narrow way initially. What were the technical things I needed to know, and what were the things I needed to learn as a manager and then as a leader? I would never have thought to find a mentor.

I realized the shift toward a growth mindset came when I started mentoring and working with other mentors because I often learned seemingly unlikely things. When I read Dweck's book, I understood and articulated this shift more profoundly. My exponential growth came when I shifted from knowing what I thought I needed to learning incredible things and how someone in another function thought about issues and challenges.

For example, I had a mentee who worked in customer experience, sometimes referred to as customer service; her challenges made me think about how that impacted my organization. As a financial executive, I didn't routinely think about customers. I gained some sensitivity to what it was to be a health care professional during COVID-19. What does it feel like to be from a different country, race, ethnicity, or sexual orientation than the norm in an organization?

I heard a talk about mentoring— it was more about who you are rather than what you do. I think this gets to the core of the mentoring mindset. In response to one of my LinkedIn posts on mentoring, someone responded, "Mentoring is who I am...not what I do." I loved it! What does it take to shift mentoring from what you do to who you are? I think that comes down to your mindset.

I researched traits of a great mentor—nowhere did I see "C-level executive," "MBA," "fifteen-plus years' experience," "sales experience," or anything about what mentors do. What I found was words that describe *who* mentors are. They are good listeners; they are trustworthy and honest. They have empathy, sensitivity, and patience. They are collaborative, and they have a growth mindset.

Paru Radia is an executive strategist, business consultant, entrepreneur coach, and one of my go-to mindset mentors. She suggests the right mindset in mentoring starts with examining your motives. For mentors, are you doing it to make a positive impact, or are you doing it to look good? For mentees, are you doing it to check off a box to say you have a mentor, or are you looking to grow and learn?

As we spoke, I wanted to explore the opposite side of the equation: the mentor's motivation. And I thought a bit about my motivations. Were all of my reasons for mentoring based on mutual learning? I'm pretty proud of the title "mentor" ...maybe too proud? I suspect I've sometimes been more enamored with the actual mentoring than in what my partner was getting out of the relationship.

Paru also spoke about finding a mentor who stretched you and was different from you. She shared the story of a mentee—a relatively junior woman (let's call her Flo) who was shocked her mentor in a company-sponsored program was a man. Flo shared, "I wanted a mentor who was a woman so she would understand my perspective." I believe a mentee should get the kind of mentor she wants. She was matched with a guy who happened to be the chief technology officer (CTO—so organizationally, a pretty big guy). Paru counseled her mentee that in this case, and in most, "different" can be good. It could also work in her favor to have someone so senior looking out for her, if he does, of course.

My coach, Pat Romboletti, often says, "Different is better than better."

The late Stephen R. Covey writes in *The 7 Habits of Highly Effective People* about valuing differences; not just the physical, male/female, young/old, and white/black, but valuing social, mental, and emotional differences. These differences create an environment that is truly fulfilling for each person. Other chapters will dive deeper into gender and race/ethnicity issues.

As a mentor, what are your motivations? Are you most comfortable with a "mini me," a partner who is a former version of yourself? Or do you value, even seek, someone who can learn from your mistakes?

I was guilty of being too prescriptive regarding mentees. I co-founded a program that grew out of a women's employee resource group, and our first phase included mostly women mentees (fifty women and five men) while most of the mentors were male. We soon realized excluding a significant percentage of our potential mentees from our program was somewhat hypocritical if we strive for inclusion. Yet, I favored mentees who were women; I was a righteous feminist. At some point, I realized if I valued diversity, I needed to be gender-neutral when mentoring. I needed a mindset shift. While the focus of this book and my efforts is women mentoring women, there are benefits to cross-gender mentoring to support inclusivity.

Mindset isn't set or constant. It's something to be checked daily; I know people who set alarms on their phones to check their mindset. I have added a mindset check to my mentoring prep time as I write this. There are plenty of tips to reset your mindset. Do you phone a friend (my personal favorite)? Listen to great music? Closely related to phone a friend, do you surround yourself with people with great mindsets? I know a woman who watches the same gratitude video first thing *every* morning. She's one of the most positive people I know.

Motivational speaker Jim Rohn famously said, "You are the average of the five people you spend the most time with." Those closest to us are greatly influence us. It affects our thinking, self-esteem, and decisions. More importantly, you are likely one of those five people in your mentee's life. Are you surrounding yourself with the right people to support you as a mentor? Is your mindset where it should be? Have you checked your mindset before you speak to your partner? Have you supported your mentee in working on her mindset for your mentoring sessions and her life? Resetting your mindset can be as easy as taking a breath or getting some water.

So, take a breath! Next, we will look at mentoring and gender, which has gotten even more interesting in our post-#MeToo world.

PART 2

MENTORING TOPICS

CHAPTER 4

GENDER

"Behind every successful woman is a tribe of other successful women."

UNKNOWN

Many of my mentees were matched with me through formal programs. Some specifically asked for a woman. In an initial meeting with one of them, my newly minted mentee initially thought I was perfect but wondered, "Do I need a male mentor? My boss and his bosses are men, and most of my colleagues are men." She continued, "Do I need a mentor who is like me...or like them?"

There's a lot written about men as allies, mentors, and sponsors, but perhaps that takes a narrow view of leadership—not unlike Superman saving Lois Lane. This book focuses on women mentoring women, but much of the guidance works for anyone mentoring anyone. However, in mentoring, gender can be an issue, good or bad. Let's take a look at gender and mentoring.

I received a call from a mentee; we'll call her Jen. We were "matched" over a decade ago as part of a formal program, and she specifically asked for her mentor to be a woman. As mentors, we could not state our preferences, but we could suggest what kind of mentee we could help most. I preferred to mentor women (recall, I founded the women's initiative that led to the mentoring program).

Jen's been with the same company for over a decade and received a promotion in the past year. A senior woman in her organization, let's call her Ann, contacted Jen. Ann was hiring for a newly created role reporting directly to her (Ann is a fabulous woman). Jen gave it some thought, and we talked about it. While the role had a certain appeal, it didn't fit in with Jen's career plans, and it was a lateral move (no additional responsibility). My mentee called Ann back and told her while she was flattered with the outreach, she didn't think the role was right for her at this time.

Jen and I also discussed whether she should tell her male boss, and ultimately, she did. Just a reminder, Ann approached Jen about the role, and Jen decided *not* to pursue it. Her boss's response was remarkable: "well, you are ambitious!" in a less than optimistic tone. Jen pondered that for two days and finally called me on a Sunday afternoon and asked me if I had "fifteen minutes." I laughed. We have never had a fifteen-minute conversation; we struggled to keep to our planned sixty minutes. I settled in for our discussion.

Based on past conversations, it appeared Jen's manager wasn't the most enlightened guy around, but this comment seemed strange to me in many ways. My first statement/question was, "I thought ambition was a good thing?" I admire and try to hire and promote ambitious people. I always thought of Jen as ambitious, and I suspect she would describe herself the same way (I should have asked). So perhaps it was a compliment? Not likely.

We talked a little more; we tried to find some positives. At least Jen's manager wanted to keep her; he could have been too enthusiastic about pursuing another role.

We wrapped up that part of the conversation and decided there wasn't anything else to do at that time. Jen's conversation with her boss and our subsequent mentoring chat might prepare her for future discussions. My partner seemed okay with the resolution, but I felt unsatisfied.

I'd encountered similar situations in the past when a woman does something very similar to a man. For example, a man and a woman both ask for a promotion. The guy is perceived as "good" ambitious, and the woman is "too" ambitious, or in a not so good way.

In Jen's case, she didn't do anything all that ambitious—she responded to another manager's inquiry. We continued with our agenda items, including her non-profit efforts. Jen's volunteer work energizes her, but she says, "They are working me hard." Boundaries are a common topic for us, but we'd only considered work boundaries in the past.

I should have suggested she get a male perspective on this conversation on ambition. We were assuming her boss had a "male" response. Was I giving her "woman" guidance? Would a gender-balanced exploration have suited her better? I think so.

I received another call from Jen a few weeks later. Ann reached out again and offered to be Jen's sponsor. Her new sponsor sees her ambition positively.

Jen's goal is a senior leadership position, not unlike many women. She has a mentor, a sponsor, and potentially a new job, but she and women overall still have a way to go.

Despite gains, women are still underrepresented in senior leadership roles; we may have cracked the glass ceiling, but the ceiling is still there. In a recent report, "The State of Women in Corporate America," McKinsey & Company reports, despite COVID-19, women's representation had improved across most of corporate America at the end of 2020.

The report said at the start of 2021, women represent:

- 48 percent of the entry-level workforce (up 5 percent in five years).
- 41 percent at management levels (again up from five years earlier by 9 percent).
- 35 percent by the senior manager/director level (up 6 percent over five years).
- 30 percent (again up 6 percent in five years) by the VP level.
- 27 percent of the SVP level.
- 24 percent of the C-suite roles.

At the C-suite level; we see the most significant increase: a 27 percent improvement over five years. C-suite (or C-level) roles are the most senior roles in an organization, like the chief executive officer, chief financial officer, or chief marketing officer. Mentoring can play a role in getting more women into senior positions. Curiously, while women are climbing the ladder, mentoring of women by men has decreased. We need to maintain that pace of improvement at the C-level and increase it at lower levels to feed the pipeline to the C-suite.

Lynn Sontag is the CEO and owner of Menttium Corporation in Minneapolis. Menttium celebrated its thirtieth anniversary in 2021. When Menttium launched its flagship program in 1991 to help women move into leadership positions, almost *all* of their volunteer mentors were men. Now fast forward to 2022, when Menttium has both women and men enrolled as mentees in their programs, over 70 percent of their mentors are women. I am honored to have been a repeat mentor with Menttium.

Women are mentoring women, and we need more women to mentor—to feed the leadership pipeline—and get more mentees and mentors into senior roles. But we need more mentors overall, men and women. While this book focuses on women mentoring women, my overarching goal is to encourage more mentoring.

The flip side of having a mentoring partner who is the same gender is a woman may want a mentor who is a man (or vice versa) *because* most of the people she works with are men, and she wants to see things from a different perspective. A woman considers behavior as assertive, yet a man might view it as aggressive or even something that starts with a B and rhymes with witch. Recall the story earlier in this chapter. Does ambition look different in men and women? Or *to* men and women?

There are times when gender may play a role in achieving the development goals of the mentee. Juggling the job and family demands may challenge a working parent. Things make be a bit different for a single moms or dads, especially only parents or the only parent providing care. A widowed dad may be a better partner for a woman raising her children on her own than a single dad who sees his kids every other weekend.

In mentoring and leadership, gender sensitivity is essential. I pursued a role within my company. The company and my manager were supportive of the move. He was a good boss and an all-around great person. He shared this pearl of wisdom: "If you and a guy are equally qualified for a job, he will get it. You need to be 10 percent better." He reassured me I was more than 10 percent better than the other candidate. As I said, he was a good guy.

The advice may have been genuine. I did not get the job, and I don't think it had anything to do with my gender. I took away being 10 percent better than anyone (male or female) would give me a better chance in any role. Still, perhaps he didn't frame that as well as possible.

Let's hear about a woman who mentored a woman contemplating a career change—with a better approach.

MJ Thomas is a former FBI officer, former law enforcement officer, former military officer, and a serial mentor. She says she now "makes boats" in Maine. Translation: MJ is the director of security at General Dynamics–Bath Iron Works. Bath Iron Works is a full-service shipyard specializing in designing, building, and supporting complex surface combatants for the US Navy. "Makes boats" is an understatement; MJ has a big job at a complex organization. As I spoke to her via Zoom, models and photos of ships were everywhere.

Mentees and all humans sometimes blow problems out of proportion. A good mentor can help diffuse the situation and get the partner focused on the reality of the situation and moving forward. A great mentor can take that a step beyond and ask, "What can we learn from this?"

A woman, let's call her Beth, needed guidance on career options and approached MJ. Beth was contemplating a career change because she had a lousy boss and had broken her finger (MJ wiggled her index finger on the screen). The typical mentor would probably focus on the bad boss situation. Not MJ, because she thought deeper. She focused on the broken finger.

I was confused. A broken finger is an annoyance in many ways; typing is more complex, personal grooming becomes difficult. The mentee was a professional woman. Was this mentee making more of this than it was? Could a broken finger be career-ending if you aren't doing manual labor or heavily reliant on your hands, maybe as a surgeon or an artist?

I unconsciously donned my "mentoring hat" and framed the issue around my experiences, the experiences of other professional women, and my brother, the former mechanic. As leaders, our success depends on our heart and mind; physical abilities should be irrelevant.

Our Zoom meeting continues, and MJ makes a gun shooting motion on the screen. She went on to say, "It was her trigger finger."

Suddenly, I got it. "Not all fingers are alike!" I thought. If my "trigger finger" isn't at 100 percent, it may take me longer to do my job or get dressed. Perhaps there are a few more typos, but it's not a matter of life or death. Women fear the perception of "not tough enough," and indeed, for those in careers that require guns, that pressure is more pronounced. If firing a weapon is part of your job, your trigger finger must be fully functional.

Fortunately, MJ had a unique tool in her mentoring tool belt. She sustained a far more severe injury involving multiple body parts in her shoulder, arm, and hand. MJ shared with Beth, "I planned to fully recover from my injuries. If not, I would simply learn to shoot with my other hand" (not so simple for most of us). MJ did make a full recovery. MJ advised her mentee a broken finger was not necessarily a career-limiting problem, even for someone in law enforcement. MJ was a living example of making a full recovery from an injury. She shared setbacks are part of any job and rebounding from setbacks, whether a bad boss or a broken finger, was key to career advancement.

She encouraged Beth she could have a successful career if she was resilient.

The meeting ended without further conversation, and MJ thought Beth needed some time to process the feedback.

Perhaps going more profound here, was the broken finger a trigger in a way? Was it a message from the universe that it was time for a career change? Now that's a topic a mentor could dig into in a subsequent conversation. A great mentor might think, "What's my trigger finger?" Does my mentee have any "trigger fingers"? Or going even further, where am I using a surface problem to camouflage another? I've often seen this with employees complaining about their commute to work; once we get more profound, the underlying problem with the commute is they are no longer motivated to make it as the job is unsatisfying.

We don't know how this story ends. MJ never heard back from this mentee. Perhaps the best thing MJ did was not follow up when she didn't hear back from Beth. If the mentee was not open to guidance and thought one conversation could address the challenge of a potential career change, perhaps she wasn't really committed to career advancement. MJ could model resilience and provide mentoring, but Beth needed to do the work to recover from both her physical injury and her poor supervisor. Ultimately, both partners were responsible for their growth and development.

What did I learn from this story, and how can we apply it to our mentoring? A mentee should choose a mentor based on her, the mentee's, needs. The "trigger finger" mentee chose well; she found in MJ a one-time mentor who understood her challenge from her perspective. In this case, seeking a woman mentor probably made sense, but it might have been helpful also to get a male perspective (the mentee may have done that) since it was a male-dominated organization.

I know hundreds of fabulous mentors, and only a handful could have dealt with this situation. What will I do in the future if I have a mentee who has broken her trigger finger? I will refer her to MJ or someone who can appreciate her challenge.

Reflecting on Marissa Fernandez's guidance on the mirror (pun intended), where she suggested mentors use a mirror to have mentees reflect on their challenges, there may be times when you need to hand the mirror to someone else to get the correct reflection.

MIXING IT UP

Kim Scott, the author of *Radical Candor* and *Just Work*, shared some wisdom from her Just Work co-founder Trier Bryant. Trier suggests women should have mentors who are both women and men (and multiple races) to discuss the same topics to ensure what they are experiencing is or is not biased.

I decided to do a little informal research and polled my LinkedIn network about their preference for mentoring relationships. Almost two hundred people responded—but clearly, there is nothing scientific about this poll; I wanted to explore what people do in their mentoring relationships.

An eyeball of the results indicated the group included men and women. Better than half, 55 percent, of the respondents have a mix of genders in their mentoring relationships. Both mentors and mentees in this group believed that variety was the spice of life and that partners from various genders would result in a better balance and, more significant, broader learning. So do I! They support Trier Bryant's approach.

Curiously, 24 percent of the respondents preferred to partner with mentees or mentors of the same gender. This group was overwhelmingly women, with most of the comments indicating that's where women mentors felt they could add the most value. Only 7 percent of the respondents preferred partners of another gender; again, the group was a mix of men and women. Yes, I know that doesn't add up to 100 percent—14 percent fell into the "it depends" category; I'm one of those people.

The poll and comments made me think a bit about my own mentoring, particularly about my "why." Why did I mentor and why did I mentor primarily women? Why did I co-found and co-lead a program? The comments about women mentoring other women, where the women mentors felt they brought the most value, raised questions for me.

On some level, it may be true some women get the most value in mentoring other women, especially if the mentee has specific issues related to gender—sexual harassment, single mom, or being the only woman in a company or group. I wonder if down deep there is something else going on—a concern we can't appropriately mentor men?

I hope not. My other thought is having mentees of different genders would lead to a broader experience for both partners, as many of my poll respondents indicated. I'll talk more about selfish mentoring in a later chapter.

One final thought, as I mentioned in the introduction: men are sometimes hesitant to mentor women in our post-#MeToo era. There is a minimal risk of sexual impropriety if the relationship is goal-driven and focused on professional development.

While I'm sure there have been some issues, I've been associated with thousands of mentoring partnerships over the years, interviewed dozens of people for this book, did some research, and have not heard of one instance of sexual impropriety in a mentoring relationship. If we apply the norms we use for other business relationships to mentoring, I think we will all be okay.

Next up, mentoring in our new normal.

CHAPTER 5

THE NEW NORMAL

"In the midst of chaos, there is also opportunity."

SUN TZU

The world has changed since January 1, 2020, and the challenges impacted mentors and mentees. From the difficulties of COVID-19 economic and financial hardships to social and racial injustice. Many mentoring relationships have been disrupted or ended, while others have launched or upgraded. For those with a growth mindset (see Chapter 3), the COVID-related challenges provided an opportunity for growth and learning. In my case, the initial months of the pandemic saw former mentees becoming my mentors. The pandemic accelerated trends that were developing—movements such as virtual mentoring.

An August 2021 article in Human Resources Executive, "Why COVID-19 Has Made Mentoring for Women a Must," suggests the pandemic has accelerated the need for mentoring for women. The article states the most significant drivers are depression and the ongoing childcare crisis.

I think it goes much further than that and positioning mentoring as a "women's issue" minimizes the need and potential impact of mentoring. I'd argue the need for mentoring is more pronounced now than it's ever been for most professionals.

I wondered what others thought, so I asked my LinkedIn network, "Has your mentoring activity changed since the beginning of the pandemic?" Here are the survey results:

- 50 percent - I'm doing more.
- 24 percent - I've changed/expanded my focus.
- 14 percent - It's about the same.
- 12 percent - I'm doing less.

The comments added details and examples:

Eugina Jordan, vice president of marketing at Parallel Wireless, shared the pandemic prompted her to launch a mentorship program at her company.

Shami Anand, a leadership coach and strategist, launched a Women's Supply Management Community in 2021. One of their goals is developing and rolling out a mentor program for women.

Deanna Johnston, a seasoned government affairs executive, answered my question about the increased need with "absolutely yes"; she's mentoring more. Michelle Stevenson, a communications executive, agreed, "I think the need (for mentoring) has increased." I agree!

Steve Fiore, area vice president at Teradata Grafton, says he has "focused on work-life balance in my conversations over the past eighteen months" (2020-2021). Work-life balance (covered in Chapter 9) became a more significant issue in 2020 for mentees.

Liliana Petrova, a customer experience visionary, thinks, "My mentoring has not changed fundamentally, but we now talk more about purpose than before. Pre-COVID-19, things were a bit more linear, and we talked strictly about work."

Denise Brosseau, CEO at the Thought Leadership Lab, said, "I think mentoring well can be critical for people going through challenging times like these. This is an important reminder for me to reach out to some of my mentees and be sure everything is okay."

As in many other areas, the pandemic accelerated trends. Virtual mentoring was becoming more common; it was now essential. Mentoring evolved to a more holistic approach to the mentee's (and mentor's) development. During the pandemic, boundaries between our professional and personal lives evaporated. COVID-19 pushed mentoring partners to go broader and deeper in their conversations—which is terrific.

Overall, I believe the COVID-19 raised the bar for mentoring—let's keep it high and look for ways to increase it a bit more.

Angela (Angie) Hoernemann was my mentoring partner in a Menttium virtual mentoring program launched in March 2019; our formal, one-year relationship ended just before the pandemic. Angie is the vice president of behavioral account management at Cigna. We had a good mentoring relationship—I think she would agree.

We positioned her for what was next and set boundaries, as she worked remotely. She works from her home in Minnesota, and we had plans to meet in person in the spring of 2020 when she would be in NYC facilitating mental health first aid for a national association. I'd never heard of mental health first aid and planned to enroll in a class. Neither that class nor our in-person meet-up ever happened.

I used the quarantine period in the spring of 2020 to reconnect with people, including Angie. Curiously enough, during our time together in 2019, we met only by phone—I suspect it was because Menttium suggested a call as part of their program launch. We took a bit leap and met on screen; I had never seen more than a photo of Angie. This meeting took place before Zoom fatigue set in. I was thrilled.

We did a general catch-up that included work, family, and dogs. We both had two pups. Then I realized while the rest of us were struggling with working remotely, Angie had been doing it for over a decade. She successfully led a team from her home and shared some tips. Perhaps more importantly, Angie was trained and experienced in mental health first aid—something we all needed. Mental health first aid is a national program to teach the skills to respond to mental illness and substance abuse signs.

Let's look at the impacts of the pandemic more broadly.

In March 2021, McKinsey published the article "Seven charts that show COVID-19's impact on women's employment" in honor of International Women's Day. The charts highlight the following:

- McKinsey's pre-COVID-19 research had never shown women opt out of the workforce at higher rates than men. From 2015 to 2019, men showed higher rates of attrition.
- Before COVID-19, women slowly made some progress in the workplace (we explored this in Chapter 4).
- COVID-19 dealt a significant setback. The effect was immediate; one out of four women considered leaving the workforce.
- Women feel more pressure at work than men (when asked if they felt consistent pressure at work). That includes pressure to work more/longer hours and feelings of burnout and exhaustion.
- The effects—both at work and home—have been the worst for women in emerging economies; this includes a wide range of issues from workplace safety to opportunities for advancement to household responsibilities.
- Acting now to improve gender equity could add thirteen trillion dollars to global GDP (gross domestic product).
- Advancing gender equity will require a focus on how work is changing.

McKinsey thinks we have work to do at many levels, and I believe mentoring can make the new normal a better normal for women and everyone.

I'll start with work-from-home/remote work. I'll dive into gender equity later in the book and discuss some of the "pressure at work" and the effects—at work and home.

VIRTUAL MENTORING IS HERE TO STAY

Over the past ten years, most of my formal mentoring has been virtual; Angie and I didn't need to adjust much with COVID-19. Angie worked remotely, and we lived in different time zones. The adjustment to virtual wasn't so seamless for many, especially the "social" people.

That's a great question to ask your partner: "What format works best for you now?" It's a great question to ask almost anyone. The most significant change for me initially was I moved from phone calls, probably because some of those relationships started pre-Zoom and some pre-iPhone, to Zoom or FaceTime. Then we moved back to phone calls in response to Zoom fatigue.

Mentoring Takeaway
You may need to adjust your meeting cadence, location, or format to suit changing situations or keep your meetings interesting.

Virtual mentoring can provide a more psychologically safe space for younger mentees (like students). In many ways, virtual mentoring is more manageable. You don't have to travel somewhere; you might have fewer distractions. Perhaps the most significant advantage of virtual mentoring is that it opens up so many partner options. You can find mentees in different countries, regions, or states, partners in other industries, and from different socio-economic groups.

You can get a little creative and perhaps have some fun virtually. In the past, you could attend a conference or talk together. That came at the cost of time and money. Consider watching a TED Talk or other talk together and discuss. I love to have my partners do a virtual "walk-around." I'm curious about their "workspace," what they see out their windows, their kids, and their dogs.

WORK FROM HOME/REMOTE WORK

"Remote work is the future of work."

ALEXIS OHANIAN, REDDIT CO-FOUNDER
AND EXECUTIVE CHAIRMAN

While remote work, work from home, and flexible work arrangements may be an excellent option for many women and men, there are challenges.

Zoom fatigue, also known as virtual meeting fatigue, is the feeling of exhaustion that often occurs after attending a series of virtual meetings. In the early days of the pandemic, most of us thought we'd be living in a Zoom world for a few weeks or months, not a few years, or possibly forever for some.

In addition, the boundaries between our work lives and personal lives blur. Our dining room table may now be the center of both. As I mentioned in the story that started this chapter, this is one area where both mentoring partners were experiencing the pandemic for the first time together—an opportunity for peer mentoring; we'll figure this out together. In my case, it presented an opportunity for reverse mentoring; two of my mentees are more experienced with remote work than I was. I was not alone.

Mentoring partners can share best practices and lessons learned—and perhaps opt for a virtual walk. Meet by phone rather than Zoom. Maybe you could agree to meet "off hours"; enjoy a virtual glass of wine later in the day. Encourage your partner to schedule "Zoom breaks," breaks that do not involve feeding the kids lunch or running an errand. It could be a quick walk or a few minutes of cuddling with your loved one/kids/pets.

The work vs. personal boundary issue is real. I wrote this book at my dining table. I had my MacBook, planner, notebook, pen, tray with hound (as in the dog), salt and pepper shakers, candle and plant, and a box of replacement parts for my Roomba. My world collided physically and otherwise.

Partners can help each other set appropriate boundaries; one size does not fit all. I'm a morning person, so an early meeting isn't a problem. I'm most productive before noon. My problem was my evening shut down. My coach suggested I schedule it on my calendar, like a meeting. I now have thirty minutes blocked after my last meeting or five p.m., whichever is later. I close my laptop at that point (sometimes I put it in the closet).

I've asked my mentoring partners and others to hold me accountable. After hours, they are to publicly humiliate me if I respond to a message, e-mail, etc. My fabulous cohort partners did one better; they offered alternatives to evening activities during the pandemic. My goal was *not* to trade my Mac screen for a television screen. I started doing needlepoint while listening to audiobooks. I get away from my laptop and my granddaughter will love the unicorn needlepoint I'm making. For me, setting boundaries meant getting away from a screen; it may be different for you or your partner.

Even as we return to the "new normal," we deal with the lingering impact on our families and ourselves. Women continue to bear most of the child care burden, which has become more significant in the pandemic. Women disproportionately take charge, whether it's your parent who is anxious about getting a vaccine/booster or seeing a doctor, or a child who is suddenly back to virtual school after an outbreak of COVID. Mentoring partners can support each other with these challenges. That starts with addressing the issue. From there, partners can explore strategies to deal with these challenges in the short and long term. It may also be helpful to analyze whether the mentee's current function/organization/industry is supportive of flexible work arrangements.

THE MOVE TO TECHNOLOGY AND AUTOMATION

COVID-19 accelerated the reliance on technology and automation and heightened the Zoom fatigue just mentioned. Here again, reverse mentoring or a traditional mentoring partnership with a younger, likely more tech-savvy mentee can be beneficial. It's not just learning about the latest app, but the language that goes with the tech. We all remember the tech dinosaurs who took to the app "to Twitter." Partners can use mentoring to explore new technology. There's nothing like a good screen-share to work through the quirks of a new app. I did that with a mentoring partner when I first used Canva.

Mentoring is an excellent opportunity for both partners to assess their tech and other skill sets. Are there skills you need to advance in the post-COVID-19 world? For example, a person might be extraordinarily skilled at in-person communication but loses her charisma on a phone call. Do pithy text messages result in a thread of similarly terse messages over several hours when a quick call was more appropriate?

Technology allows access to various platforms to enable mentoring outside of your usual orbit. Sarah Bierenbaum, a customer success executive, shared, "I've definitely started mentoring more, both through organic industry connection and through the Catalyst Software coaching corner that pairs CS (customer success) leaders with mentees each quarter."

REASSESSING PRIORITIES

Adam Grant is a best-selling author, organizational psychologist, and professor at the Wharton School of the University of Pennsylvania. He tweeted, "The Great

Resignation isn't a mad dash away from the office. It's the culmination of a long march toward freedom. Flexibility is more than choosing the place where you work. It's having the freedom to decide your purpose, your people, and your priorities." The Great Resignation refers to the roughly thirty-three million Americans who quit their jobs since the spring 2021, as of January 2022.

Career advancement has always been an essential part of mentoring, and what career advancement looks like has changed. The pandemic accelerated a pre-COVID-19 trend of individuals reassessing their priorities, and mentees and mentors are no exception. Many women (and men) may want to trade in the corner office for a desk in their basement. Others may be anxious to swap a business lunch at a trendy restaurant for PB&J with the kids.

While many may want to explore their purpose, people, and priorities, the question is "when?" When do you have time with a workday full of meetings, Zooms, and responsibilities at home? My answer is "during your mentoring sessions." Perhaps you meet more frequently and allocate time each session to career advancement. I'll do a deeper dive in a later chapter.

How can you help your team members align their purpose and priorities with their work? It may be more than "how often do I need to be in the office?" On the flip side, mentoring partners can discuss strategies for combatting the Great Resignation. You can share ways to engage and retain your workforce.

Do you remember my mentee Gee from the introduction? She was in New York on business in early March 2020. We planned to have dinner at the South Street Seaport while in town. We met on March 3. It's almost hard to remember what things were like then.

NYC would shut down ten days later, but restaurants and stores were still open that night. I had a nasty cough and was frightening everyone around me. I stopped at the nearby Duane Reade pharmacy to buy over-the-counter medication for my cough and hand sanitizer on the way to dinner. I was successful on the former, unsuccessful on the latter. In some ways, this mentoring dinner was like countless dinners before, but at some point, the conversation turned to COVID-19, and we speculated on what it might mean for us and the world.

After over fifteen years, our relationship has morphed from traditional mentoring—with me in the mentor role— to a peer mentoring relationship. That night, Gee might not have been the mentor, but she was undoubtedly the wiser of the two of us.

I relayed my story of the trip to Duane Reade and voiced a concern that I would be unable to find *any* hand sanitizer (and remember, in the spring of 2020, we were all about hand sanitizer). Gee, always prepared, and a long-time germaphobe, gave me a small container of hand sanitizer— with a Jackson State University logo and a clip. I still have it and refilled it countless times.

Toward the end of dinner, I had a full-blown coughing fit, much to the dismay of everyone around us. I'd gotten accustomed to telling total strangers, "It's not COVID-19; I don't have a fever." When I settled down, my dear partner and now mentor said, "Michelle, you don't have COVID-19. That's your asthma cough. You need to talk to your doctor."

The most significant symptom for me is an uncontrollable cough. I'd forgotten I'd been diagnosed with severe asthma early in our relationship. I'd since gotten it under control and hadn't even considered "my" asthma was the culprit, but fortunately, Guyna remembered and left me with a follow-up task to call my doctor the next day—which I did. Within days, I was no longer terrifying strangers—or anyone else—with my cough. My partner helped me focus on health as a priority and identify the real problem. And she held me accountable to take action.

Mentoring Takeaway
The nature of your mentoring relationship may change over time and flip instantly.

LESSONS LEARNED DURING THE PANDEMIC
People spent their quiet time in various ways: some perfected "Netflix and chill," others used the quarantine period to reassess priorities and develop new habits. You might have read more, savored old movies, learned a new language, or rediscovered a love of cooking. I know mentoring partners who did exercise challenges together.

What worked about remote work and what didn't? Mentoring sessions are a fabulous time to review lessons learned from the pandemic and to plan to continue those best practices. Your mentoring partner can be your accountability partner.

TIME

I asked Eugina Jordan, vice president of Marketing at Parallel Wireless, whether she was mentoring more. I guessed she was. Her answer was, "Most definitely. I am traveling less, so I am doing more of what I enjoy doing, and mentoring is one of those things".

I realized I had done the same thing but hadn't been as thoughtful about it. We may travel less for business, and we may no longer have a commute—or at least commute on fewer days. Rather than filling your commute/travel time with more work—or social media—consider finding a new mentee or two to support them in this new world and grow yourself.

One last thought on mentoring in the new normal. Most mentoring training suggests a quick catch-up—maybe a review of highs and lows. Our new normal is a terrific time to spend a little more time diving deeper. Is your partner okay? While most mentors are not mental health professionals, they can support their partners at this challenging time with increased depression and anxiety.

I often use a juggling analogy; we are jugglers of time and effort. Are your partner's balls up in the air? And if they are, are any on fire? When is it okay to drop a ball or two? Is your mentee juggling more balls than humanly possible? Each juggler/mentee is unique; perhaps the best thing you can do is help your mentee determine which balls she should be juggling and which can she drop? Mentors are part-time firefighters. We can all do our part to prevent potential fires.

The pandemic has impacted mentoring and created a variety of challenges. It's also highlighted the benefits of mentoring, like improving communication and leadership skills and blending work and life (or creating the appropriate boundaries between them). Some people took the opportunity to up their mentoring game. Eugina shared we may have more time to do it for those of us who love mentoring. Let's use our new normal to create a new standard for mentoring, a higher bar for mentoring.

CHAPTER 6

DIVERSITY, EQUITY, AND INCLUSION

Diversity, Equity, and Inclusion (DEI) is a broad topic with lots of lively discussions and countless books, articles, podcasts, and TED talks. Mentoring and DEI (or JEDI, EDI, DEIB, or similar acronyms) could be a book. I'd love to cover all of the various dimensions of DEI, but I will focus on race/ethnicity, generational differences, neurodiversity, and intersectionality in mentoring for this book's purposes. I hope the learnings from these areas can support you with other diverse mentoring partners.

I'm a proud mentor, but here's a story that does not make me proud.

My mentee, let's call her Sarah, and I scheduled a weekend check-in. We had decided to use Zoom. She moved to a new apartment and I wanted to see it. She was running behind and returning from a storage facility; she had just picked up some items for her new place.

She zoomed in from her parked car. As usual, we started with a quick update and then moved to our standard agenda. As often happened, our conversation shifted to our different shared experiences. Sarah asked about my family and specifically about my daughter-in-laws' family dynamics. I mentioned my fabulous daughter-in-law, Anna, had different family dynamics. I commented, "They are the kind of people who have oil paintings of their ancestors hanging above the mantel. They trace their family roots to the Mayflower." My great-grandparents came through Ellis Island and did not bring art with them. Anna and I had differentiated experiences.

"Speaking of ancestors..." Sarah responds she had just picked up a photo of some family members. "Would you like to see it?" she asked.

I immediately responded, "I'd love to!"

She reached the back seat and pulled the framed sepia photo out of a box. I've seen similar images: an older woman, in this case, her great-grandmother, is seated with a small child in her lap. There is a semi-circle of women of various ages around her; Sarah points out another woman, her grandmother. The photo was a shared experience in some respects; I would soon realize how different it was.

I ask about the age of the photo. Sarah responds she isn't sure but can approximate the date based on her great-grandmother's death. I should have ended it there.

Instead, I mention that's rarely an issue in my family, particularly with anything from my father's side of the family. We have framed pictures with handwritten details under glass. My "ancestors" had a habit of writing the names, dates, and location (in one case, "the Stink Shack") of the photo...on the images. Her response floored me.

"Michelle, these women were all illiterate; they couldn't write. My great-grandmother's parents were slaves."

Sarah and I had often spoken about the similarities and differences in our families. Our families traveled across the Atlantic Ocean to the United States on ships. Her family arrived much earlier than mine did. My great grandparents came from Italy voluntarily. I should have been more conscious of the cultural lineage of slavery.

Sarah's mic drop comment was shared straightforwardly, a statement of fact rather than a commentary or emotional share. I was flabbergasted and embarrassed; I felt like I was culturally insensitive. I knew Sarah was Black and could have ancestors who were enslaved.

Our conversation reminded me that impact is more important than intention regarding DEI. I intended to create a shared experience; my impact was insensitive. Sarah knew me and that my intentions were good, so she ignored my impact. It would have been worse with someone who did know me as well. I vowed to do better.

UNCONSCIOUS BIAS

I can't move past this story without a quick comment on unconscious bias. Unconscious or implicit biases are cognitive biases that exist in our subconscious; they can be positive or negative. They impact many of our decisions by affecting our behavior. Examples of negative implicit bias are assuming women are more emotional than men or that anyone with an accent is less intelligent. A positive implicit bias assumes someone in your neighborhood has similar economic advantages or disadvantages. I'm not going to go into detail on this topic, but I want to remind you we all have these biases that impact everything we do, including mentoring.

MENTORING AND RACE/ETHNICITY

Let's return to the McKinsey study I shared in the last chapter. I'm sure it's no surprise while the representation of women decreases as they climb the corporate ladder, the numbers for women of color, or women who do not identify as white, are even worse.

Here's the breakdown for Women of Color:
- 17 percent of the workforce at the entry-level; ditto for men of color (MOC)
- 12 percent WOC at the manager level, while MOC remain constant at 17 percent
- 9 percent by senior director
- 7 percent at vice president
- 4 percent in the C-suite (executive-level leaders)

Overall, the C-suite is

- 62 percent white men
- 20 percent white women
- 13 percent MOC
- 4 percent WOC

The numbers are alarming!

If we look at just employees who identify as women, at entry levels, women of color represent 36 percent of women in the corporate workforce and only 20 percent of the women in the C-suite. The Fortune 500 didn't have a Black female CEO until 2009 when Ursula Burns became CEO of Xerox. She was also the first Fortune 500 female CEO to succeed another woman.

A 2015 study in *The Journal of Community Psychology* studied Latinx youth and found cross-race mentoring is associated with reductions in perceived racism. It further found having just one mentoring relationship with a mentor of a different race made a difference. Casual mentoring doesn't work well here.

Many Americans and people around the globe are increasingly fighting to dismantle racism and systematic injustice. Mentors of all races are in a unique position concerning mentoring underrepresented people of all ages, from school-aged kids to entry-level employees to leaders looking to break into the C-suite.

Just as some men may be hesitant to mentor women in the post #MeToo era, many white leaders are reluctant to mentor partners of another race based on fear of saying or doing the wrong thing or not knowing everything. Perhaps the first thing to acknowledge in mentoring is you may say or do something you will regret and if your mentoring partners are anything like mine, they will be more than forgiving. The next big "aha" is you don't know everything, nor does your mentee expect you to know everything or even more than she does in some areas.

A cross-racial mentoring relationship provides an excellent opportunity for both partners to glimpse what it's like to walk in someone else's stilettos and explore and work on your own biases, conscious or unconscious. What assumptions are you making based on your partner's race? What parts of your identity, such as my ancestors who were schooled and literate, are you assuming in your partner? Or in others?

One last thought on mentoring and race. Mentees and mentors often want their partners to mirror themselves; someone who looks like them or has a similar background. For example, I want another salesperson, Black woman, single parent, trans woman, fill in the blank. Similarity bias is the preference or tendency to appreciate people like us. We think we are more likely to get along with others who are the same as us.

A diverse group of mentoring partners provides the most significant opportunity for growth and learning for mentees and mentors, but there are some "math" challenges. As we've seen from the data in this chapter and the last, the number of people of color and women of color drops as we move up the corporate ladder. There are not enough women (or men) of color to mentor all people of color in the workforce.

On top of that, many of these senior women are already overburdened. They lead other race-related initiatives such as ERGs (employee resource groups) and serve on diversity initiatives. It gets even worse when we layer on intersectionality: potential mentors who are women and Black, lesbian, Latina, or underrepresented. The word I hear most often from these women is "exhausted."

A word of caution to those in well-represented primarily white groups when considering a mentor of an underrepresented group. I encourage you to respect people's time and think about what you need in a mentor. Perhaps a conversation or two could serve your needs rather than a full-blown mentoring relationship. And for mentors, men and women, in well-represented groups with mentees of color, this may be an excellent opportunity to open up your professional network to your mentee(s).

MENTORING AND GENERATIONAL DIFFERENCES (AGE)

Purdue University Global has a terrific infographic depicting the five generations in the workforce today. Here's a reminder of those generations and some generalizations around them.

Traditionalists: (born 1926–1945):

- Comprise two percent of the workforce.
- Shaped by the Great Depression, World War II, radio, and television.
- Tend to be dependable, straightforward, discreet, and loyal.

Baby Boomers: (born 1946–1964):

- Account for a quarter of workers.
- 65 percent of this group plan to work past the age of sixty-five.
- Ten thousand reach retirement age every day.
- Shaped by the Vietnam War and the civil rights movement.
- Characterized as optimistic, competitive, workaholic, and team-oriented. That certainly describes many of my generational peers and me.

Generation X: (born 1965–1980):

- Represent a third of the current workforce.
- Shaped by the AIDS epidemic, the fall of the Berlin Wall, and the dot-com boom.
- Tend to be flexible, informal, skeptical, and independent as a group. Most start-up founders (55 percent) are Gen Xers.
- By 2028, they will outnumber Boomers.

Millennials: (born 1981–2000):

- Make up the most significant percentage of workers at 35 percent.
- Will make up 75 percent of the workforce by 2025.

- Tend to be competitive, achievement-oriented (like Boomers), civic, and open-minded.
- Shaped by the Internet, 9/11, and Columbine.

Generation Z: (born 2001 or later):
- Five percent of the workforce.
- Progressive, global, entrepreneurial, and less focused.
- Had access to technology from a young age (some would argue too young).
- Shaped by the Great Recession and life after 9/11.

There's certainly a diversity of influences, communication preferences, and motivations between and within the generations.

Nicole Smart is a DEI architect, founder of Smart EDI Solutions LLC, New York University adjunct professor, and public speaker. She's also my go-to person on everything DEI, and her surname suits her perfectly. I asked Nicole about DEI and mentoring. She suggested generational differences are an often overlooked but essential aspect of DEI—and it might be one of the more fruitful areas for mentoring.

As a Boomer, I count on my younger mentoring partners—it's been a while since I've had an older mentoring partner—to keep me current on business trends and essential technology advancements, such as using a calendar app to make scheduling our sessions easier. Reverse or mutual mentoring is ideally suited to support generational diversity; we often generalize on the characteristics or motivations (I just did); mentoring can help us get to the "why" for an individual and their age.

Cross-generational mentoring can support boomers against ageism. A younger mentoring partner can nudge their partner to use current technology and language. Have you been there? You're in a meeting or on Zoom and someone of another generation or culture uses a term or phrase you don't understand. You either pull out your phone and google it immediately or wait until after the meeting and check it out—lest someone discovers your secret! I experienced this in a client meeting. A woman used the phrase "whatever blows your skirt up." My mind wandered between the vision of Marilyn Monroe in the promo shot for the film *The Seven Year Itch* and "that sounds sexist to me." If that phrase came up in a mentoring conversation, I could have asked my partner for the definition.

Most of us deal with all five generations in our workplace—or at least a few. Mentoring can help us explore generational differences and flex our communication to suit others. Are you surrounded by millennials you don't understand? Perhaps the answer is a millennial mentee or mentor. Or you are a GenX Founder who just hired a Boomer on your leadership team, and it feels like a big sister relationship.

MENTORING AND NEURODIVERSITY

Neurodiversity is an angle I hadn't thought about until I had a conversation with Kathryn Parsons, chief digital operations officer at MACH19 Digital in New York. She describes herself as "born non-verbal autistic" and overcame her challenges to become a speaker on neurodiversity, LGBTQ+ inclusion, and digital transformation.

Neurodiversity refers to variation in the human brain regarding sociability, learning, attention, mood, and other mental functions in a non-pathological sense. It is a non-visible disability.

As I spoke to Kathryn via Zoom, I thought I only knew one other person who was neurodiverse, then I realized I likely knew more. My ignorance certainly wasn't helping in my communication or my growth.

Kathryn shared her insight on mentoring, managing, and working with individuals who are neurodiverse. The first is to be aware they may miss typical social cues and expect certain things. One example is a person looking us straight in the eyes when they speak to us. That can be challenging for someone who is neurodiverse. Kathryn uses a workaround of looking at something behind a person. A person who is neurotypical may interpret a partner's failure to look straight into their eyes as a sign of lack of honesty or transparency. It may not be.

On a video call, she focuses on something near the camera on her device (which is an excellent hack for all of us). A mentoring partner should be cautious when using sarcasm, as a partner who is neurodiverse may take the comment literally. Again, this advice can serve others as well. Often, a partner from another culture or for whom English is a second language may miss nuances in communication. A mentor should ensure a safe space, emotionally and physically, for her partner. Physical space can be a more significant issue for those on the spectrum when noise may overstimulate them. They may be sensitive to touch. Kathryn suggests the easiest solution is to ask; again, excellent guidance overall.

In the May/June 2017 edition of *The Harvard Business Review,* an article says companies can use neurodiversity as a competitive advantage. Employees on the spectrum tend to be hard-working and wizards at data. Estimates are that one in 42 boys are autistic and one in 189 girls: in the war for talent, why would companies or managers want to exclude this population because they perceive neurodiverse employees as "different"?

Kathryn suggested finding a common interest with a partner who is neurodiverse is helpful. While I've never had a mentoring partner who is neurodiverse, or I didn't realize it, there is a gentleman on the spectrum in my extended family.

A few years ago, one of my Thanksgiving duties was driving "Uncle Jim" (not my actual uncle or even a blood relative, but his name is Jim) for Thanksgiving. He is a person who is neurodiverse. I admit I wasn't sure what we'd talk about; we seemingly had little in common, or so I thought, and my discomfort heightened when we had some communication and GPS issues with the pickup.

I am a classic rock fan, and I listen to the radio (the old school kind) all the time, especially when I drive. I had my favorite station—Q104.3—on when Uncle Jim got into the car. I turned the volume down as he was clicking his seat belt. Uncle Jim yelled out, "Turn that back up; this is my favorite radio station!" We had a great conversation about music. We did have something in common, after all. Mentoring partnerships can build from both commonalities and differences.

INTERSECTIONALITY AND MENTORING

Intersectionality is "the network of connections between social categories such as race, class, and gender, especially when this may result in additional disadvantage or discrimination" per the *Oxford Learner's Dictionaries.*

In the article "Intersectional Mentorship: A Model for Empowerment and Transformation" published by the Cambridge University Press, the authors' model "moved beyond traditional approaches in which mentors provide based on their own experiences" which may be very different and perhaps not very relevant to your mentee.

This approach asks mentors to shift and be more self-aware of their structural positions, where their role sits in an organization, and do the necessary work to understand their mentees and their experiences.

The authors, Nadia E. Brown of Purdue University and Celeste Montoya of the University of Colorado Boulder, argue this intersectional approach to mentoring "provides better support to those at the intersection of multiple marginalities" (for example, if the mentee is a woman and Black). The model holds mentors whose structural positions provide more significant protection or advantage accountable to essentially ignore those advantages. The mentor's identity is less important than an intersectional orientation. For example, if both partners are marketing professionals of different races, the mentoring should focus on racial differences rather than functional similarities.

Here's an illustration of several of the DEI subjects I've explored.

Mariana Saddakni is a digital strategy and brand innovation leader at AT&T. She was born in Argentina and lived the first half of her life there. She received a Bachelor of Arts from The University of Buenos Aires. She came to the United States to study design and innovation technology at Parsons School of Design, where she earned a Master of Fine Arts and has been a New Yorker since. She "started all over" when she moved to New York and was labeled "a Latina," which didn't mean anything. Her mother is a second-generation Italian Roman Catholic; her dad is a first-generation Syrian, Lebanese, and Christian Orthodox. Mariana was raised with both cultures and speaks multiple languages. Her husband is German Jewish.

Mariana has worked in New York since earning her master's degree and has advanced in her career. She also started a family. Upon passing a milestone birthday, she received an evaluation as neurodiverse. There is evidence of increased autism in perimenopausal and postmenopausal women. She felt she had "to get [herself] in a box."

Mariana summarized her challenges in dealing with some people, "It's not about being white. It's about being narrow, neurotypical. Because a neurodiverse person who is

Black, he'll understand how to create connections that are beyond race and color."

When I asked for guidance for mentoring mentees who are neurodiverse, she replied, "First, inform yourself. Educate yourself like you are also educating us." That education involves both learning about neurodiversity and the actual mentoring topics. You may need to adjust your language or approach in your communication.

Share things such as what you do and how you deal with people from different cultures. Neurodiversity is a form of diversity; while communicating with a mentee who is neurodiverse may be new to you, you have likely mentored someone different in some way. Freely share how you bridged the differences.

Further, Mariana adds, "If you come from a place of respect, empathy, and acceptance, you will never cross anyone. Be discerning of where the other person is allowing you to go." Again, you will need to be very explicit; don't assume your partner knows you are empathetic. You can say, "I know we have different backgrounds, and I am striving to be respectful and empathetic. I may need your help and input. I want to be open with you, but I respect your boundaries. I need your help in telling me what areas you are comfortable discussing."

As we wrapped up our conversation, I thought, "Isn't that great advice for all mentoring relationships, all relationships?" Be clear in your communication, do your homework on your partner's background—socially, culturally, and professionally—and agree on boundaries in your conversation. Even a mentee who seems to be like you on the surface is different in more ways. It may be the most incredible opportunities for mutual growth are in your differences rather than your similarities.

If your mentee is at an intersection, you may need to consider which attribute is most relevant in the particular challenge. For instance, a mentee shared she received feedback on her apparent lack of executive presence. On the surface, it might have appeared her challenge was she was a woman on a male-dominated leadership team, or her heavy accent or curly hair were perceived as unprofessional (I have heard all). We couldn't figure out the specific issue, so she asked her boss for more detailed feedback. It turns out the problem was her casual nature on Zoom meetings—nothing to do with diversity.

SUMMARY

At the beginning of this chapter, I wrote I couldn't explore all aspects of DEI mentoring, but I wanted to give you some aspects to ponder. Many of the thoughts and guidance in this chapter apply to any mentoring relationship; don't make assumptions, be clear in your communication, and ask questions.

I don't think I know anyone who doesn't want to support DEI initiatives, and we often think we need to make significant moves. While mentoring may not seem essential and bold, I believe it's something each of us can do to advance DEI. Even if you are a college student, you can mentor a high school student (that's how I got my start).

In 2021, I completed a certificate program on Diversity, Equity, and Inclusion in the Workplace through the University of South Florida Muma College of Business. The suggestion that struck me the most was to do one thing. Sometimes, we can do so many things we are overwhelmed and do nothing. Could your One Thing for DEI be mentoring? Or to find a partner who is diverse in some way? I hope so.

Next, we will explore selfish mentoring.

CHAPTER 7

SELFISH MENTORING

"Caring for yourself is not self-indulgent. It's an act of survival."

AUDRE LORDE

Put your oxygen mask on first.

Most people think mentoring is an entirely selfless act, but we can be better mentors if we become selfish. I learned to be appropriately selfish from my mentees.

Here's an example.

"Stop me before I volunteer again," the magnet proclaimed. It illustrated a '50s-era blonde woman with a bright smile and brighter eyes. She poses in a green dress with a Peter Pan collar in front of her awninged porch. I thought, "Certainly not me" when looking at the woman.

The magnet was a "parting gift" from Rachel Nyswander Thomas, who was leaving The McGraw Hill Companies. I hired her almost four years earlier. During the interview process, I somehow forgot to inform her I was pursuing another job within the company and she would have a new manager by the end of the year. I would continue to lead the women's employee resource group Women's Initiative for Networking and Success (WINS) and the mentoring program. While I was no longer Rachel's boss, I was "promoted" to Rachel's mentor, a new, better role (I still proudly occupy that role).

We were seated in my office in "Mahogany Row," the executive section of the headquarters for McGraw Hill Education in New York City. Behind me, the Empire State Building was visible to the east. This meeting was our last during her tenure at McGraw Hill, and I knew we wouldn't see each other in person for a while. It was bittersweet; I was thrilled she was starting a new role as a vice president in Washington, DC, a long-time goal we had discussed on many occasions. Still, I like Rachel and knew I would see much less of her in the future.

We chuckled about the magnet and talked about her new role and transitioning from her current position. At the time, I thought the gift was a joke; I now realize that was a mentoring moment for me and I was too unselfish to see it. Or maybe I was too selfish to see it?

I was referred to as a "mentoring diva" by my colleagues; I had co-founded and co-led multiple mentoring programs, led mentoring training sessions, and had become a thought leader on mentoring. I was a mentoring expert, but I couldn't see, or perhaps I couldn't accept, mentoring when it was seated on the other side of my desk behind a closed door. Rachel was a trusted and caring partner, and I couldn't get out of my mentor box. I was focused on Rachel and her future, as I always was in mentoring sessions.

A few weeks later, I was on a flight bound for Mexico City, on my home away from home—recall the "kiss everyone" story, and found the magnet in my tote. I smiled and thought, "Was Rachel trying to tell me something?" and "Was the something related to mentoring?" I certainly talked about mentoring all the time. I had learned a lot in formal mentoring training, from reading, from my mentees, and from other mentors. I love sharing what I've learned—isn't that an essential component of mentoring?

What Rachel, chief operating officer of Trustworthy Accountability Group, realized at the time was I was a compulsive over-giver, which impacted me personally and professionally. I was almost addicted to giving my time, money, and effort. I grew up with "it's better to give than receive."

Did I take the suggestion from the refrigerator magnet and Rachel to heart? Not initially.

Fast forward from the gifting meeting. I was in a career crisis; my beloved boss, Rik Kranenburg, and his boss left McGraw Hill Education. While I technically still had a role, it wasn't clear where I fit in the new organization. I was devastated about losing one of my best bosses ever; the most significant factor in taking that role was Rik. He was the first (and only) person to put me in a position to lead a business—twice. I feared I would take a big step backward in my career.

I sat at my desk on Mahogany Row with Joan Carey, then the senior director in McGraw Hill's Talent Management Center of Excellence. Joan was a poster child for the mentoring program after participating as a mentee early on and later serving as a mentor on multiple occasions. She was a repeat member of our Mentoring Program Implementation team and a mentee. I had recruited Joan for the Implementation team and encouraged her to pursue her current role.

Joan offered her "condolences on the death" of my role at McGraw Hill Education and offered some mentoring. Once again, I missed it. "It's time to practice what you preach," Joan advised. I needed to stop wallowing in fear and write the next chapter of my career. Even though Joan had reached out to me to offer her support and guidance, I automatically switched to mentor mode. Again, I was trying to be a selfless mentor and was focused only on my mentee, Joan.

Traditionally, mentoring focuses on the growth and development of the mentee, and great programs/partnerships strive for mutual learning. Most successful, repeat mentors are motivated by giving back or helping others; they have learned from past mentees. They want to learn, but it's not a goal. What if mentors got a bit more selfish and made their growth and development a stated goal of their mentoring relationships?

'IMI OLA

In the article "Selfish Mentoring," Rosa Say discusses the concept of 'imi ola and mentoring. 'Imi ola is the

Hawaiian value of personal vision; it translates to "seek life." I thought that could be a way to think about mentoring. Hawaiians practice 'imi ola in several ways that apply to mentoring:

1. To seek learning. The selfish mentor would seek knowledge for herself rather than focusing on only her mentee.
2. To think positively. 'Imi ola requires practicers to take care of themselves to bring our gifts and share more generously fully. Having a positive attitude allows the mentor to grow as part of the relationship.
3. 'Imi ola encourages us to slow down and listen to a higher source or higher guidance.

Perhaps that higher voice could be that of your mentee.

What if a selfish mentor sought out these opportunities—chances to learn and grow in areas the mentee has more knowledge or experience? Perhaps they have lived or worked in another country. Or have they worked in another industry or function? Or is your partner from another culture or generation? While they would provide mentoring on topics within their comfort zone, they would lean into seeking mentees who could provide insight outside their comfort zone. A mentor in sales who experiences friction with a colleague in finance seeks a mentee in finance to better understand the point of view of a finance leader.

Maryellen Valaitis is an adjunct professor at Piedmont Technical College, board member, retired chief human resources officer, and former mentoring "partner in crime." She shared "mentoring takes many shapes and forms" and reminded me while she loved formal mentoring programs, "mentoring shouldn't be pigeonholed."

She reminded me of a concept we developed of "drive-by mentoring" as part of a mentoring menu. In addition to more traditional mentoring that lasts over time, drive-by mentoring is more episodic and initiated by the mentee. The partners have a conversation or two about a specific topic, perhaps a potential international move or dealing with a short-term tactical issue like preparing for an annual review.

REASONS TO BE A SELFISH MENTOR.
Let's explore some "selfish" reasons to mentor:

1. Battle impostor syndrome
Impostor syndrome is a psychological pattern in which an individual doubts their skills, talents, or accomplishments and has persistent internalized fear of being exposed as a fraud.

Justina "Tia" Hooper is an officer in the United States Air Force Judge Advocate General's Corps and is an adjunct professor at the Sandra Day O'Connor School of Law at Arizona State University. She believes mentoring is very similar to teaching, especially when it comes to the feeling one receives when a mentee reaches a goal or achievement based on the guidance and recommendation. She describes it as the same feeling she gets when students grasp a subject matter in the classroom. And what better way to feel like you are a maestro than to have a mentee prove it by acting on your guidance and accomplishing their mission. Whether you are mentoring or teaching someone, you are less likely to doubt your skills or talents when you have shared them with another person who acts on them and succeeds.

2. Gain confidence

Dr. Albert Bandura, a Canadian-American psychologist, defines self-confidence as a general view of how likely you are to accomplish a specific goal based on your experience. A tremendous mentoring partnership is goal-driven. Simply maintaining and growing the mentoring relationship is an admirable goal. Achieving your goals in the mentoring relationship and seeing your mentee achieve her goals will boost your confidence. Many formal mentoring programs end with a celebration; it's an excellent idea for all mentoring partnerships.

3. Discover new strengths/interests

Sandhya Jain-Patel, is a DEI consultant, author, cultural advisor, and all-around social media goddess. "I was a mentor through Art Market Mentors and learned a ton through my mentee, Francesca Budini Gattai." Francesca helped Sandhya up her LinkedIn game, specifically in positioning her abilities. She helped her navigate Instagram regarding what Sandhya was comfortable posting and establishing boundaries to protect herself. Overall, Francesca allayed her mentor's fears around social media. I have honed my social media skills in working with Sandhya. She played it forward.

4. Learn from your mentee about your company, new industries, new points of view, or different cultures
As I climbed the corporate ladder, my roles became more global. I sought out mentees in countries/regions that were new to me as a leader. My mentees provided insight into local norms. Recall my "kiss everyone" story in the first chapter.

Sonu Goel, vice president of Thales in Virginia, found her mentees "help[ed] [her] understand organizational culture." At times, the view from the top is very different than the view elsewhere. I recall the story of the monkey sitting high up in a tree. A mentor shared she (monkey or leader) looks down and sees the tops of the other monkey's heads. They look up and see the "top" monkey's butt." A very different view indeed.

5. Expand your network
Here's a compelling example of how great mentoring relationships evolve. Rose Lanard is a Diversity, Equity, and Inclusion leader, board director, and a co-founder of mine in a mentoring program. She has stayed in touch with almost all of her mentor partners over the years. One of her partners, Charlene Butterfield—an analyst at S&P Ratings—invited her to a networking event where Rose met Charlene's father. He was—and still is—the chairman of The Carver Foundation of Norwalk, Connecticut, a non-profit dedicated to closing opportunity gaps for youth. As a direct result of that event, Rose joined the foundation's marketing committee and now is a director on Carver's board and a member of its major gifts committee. It's truly a win-win: Carver can leverage Rose's

professional skills as she gets to fulfill her personal goal of a board role meaningfully.

I've had an unusual career path and switched roles and functions every few years. I've had to get up to speed very quickly. My mentoring activities helped ease many of my career transitions (both internal and to new companies) because I had mentees in the organization who could provide insight while pursuing the role and introductions once I landed.

6. Sparking joy

Several years ago, my brilliant friend, Victoria Pau, sent me a copy of Marie Kondo's *The Life-Changing Magic of Tidying Up*. I'm not sure why she felt the need to send it to me. God knows I needed it, but she had never seen my home, and I managed to keep my office (which she had seen) in relative order.

Everyone seemed to be Kondo-ing, so I read the book (actually, I read almost any book anyone gives me). Kondo's now-signature question when deciding whether to keep a physical object is, "Does this spark joy?" Her immediate answer is, "If it does, keep it. If it does not, dispose of it."

Since then, I've thought about this quite a bit, and I have decluttered physically (moves always help). But what I've focused on is "disposing" of people and non-physical things that do not spark joy. As I thought about this book, I thought about joy and mentoring. While I'm passionate about it and love mentoring and my mentees,

I struggled with whether mentoring sparked joy for me or others.

I thought about the text from Gee about her board chair appointment. My mentee was a board chairperson; she didn't achieve her goals from years ago, she shattered them! After pride, the emotion I felt most was *joy*, pure joy!

That moment made me wonder when determining if something (or someone) sparks joy, can that be answered at a particular moment in time, or does it need to be answered over time? Think about books. I have a collection of books of various genres. One or many volumes don't spark joy on any given day. Some are not joyful books, something like *Me and White Supremacy.* The joy comes often from simply having the books around.

So, does "sparking joy" translate to mentoring? Many, if most, mentoring moments are not what we would traditionally describe as joyful. Mentoring moments can be difficult digging into thorny issues and unpacking negative baggage—professional and personal. But in the end, that one text or one smile or one learning moment makes it joyful for both partners.

7. Be seen as a talent developer/finder of great talent
Kim Scott, co-founder at Just Work and Radical Candor, shared a story about reaching out to her mentor, Sheryl Sandberg, about a potential job opportunity. That mentoring conversation led to Sheryl hiring Kim at Google. A little caution here, many formal mentoring programs

do not permit mentors to hire their mentees. Be sure to check.

Being seen as a talent developer can be particularly important if you are an individual contributor who does not manage a team but aspires to in the future. Your mentoring can give you an opportunity you may not have in your "day job."

8. Manage burnout
Burnout is a real and increasing problem for mentors and all employees. A 2021 Forbes study reports that over half—52 percent—of respondents said they were experiencing burnout. Perhaps more alarming is the number is up from 43 percent in a pre-COVID-19 survey. The statistics are worse for Gen-Xers at 54 percent, a 14 percent jump from the prior year.

What does this mean for mentors? While mentoring can bring immense satisfaction and even joy, for selfless mentors (who can't say no), the risk of burnout is real. A mentor needs to be a bit selfish and consider their well-being before taking on a mentoring opportunity. When a mentor guides a mentee on dealing with burnout, they should look in the mirror and examine their steps to avoid burnout. Mastering managing burnout as a mentor supports managing burnout in other areas of your life. Here's a chance to follow Joan's advice and "practice what you preach."

9. Rethink everything
In a 2019 LinkedIn article, "Mentoring is Extremely Selfish. Do it Immediately," Matt Flachsenhaar seems to agree

with me. He says, "Being a mentor forces you to rethink everything." He realized this after a mentee asked about including a joke in a case study. His initial response was an emphatic "no, you can't work a joke into the case study. Then he thought about it and thought, "Why can't you work a joke into the case study?" or "Why can't the case study be one well-written joke?"

Rather than asking easy questions or suggesting obvious solutions, mentoring provides an opportunity for both partners to explore alternatives. Let's say your mentee feels stalled in her current position. You could ask how that feels and suggest it was time to make a move. Or you could rethink the issue and explore what she enjoys about her role and maximize that. Or explore if she can supplement whatever is lacking by a special project or volunteer role. Then you can rethink your job.

10. Accountability
You can ask your mentee to hold you accountable for achieving your seemingly selfish goals in your partnership. Once again, you will be modeling behavior and teaching a lesson that having an accountability partner increases the probability of accomplishing a goal.

This list could be a chapter on its own, and I'm sure you can add your reasons. As I looked back on the list, a few things struck me. I wasn't alone in seeing the benefits of mentoring to mentors; there is quite a bit written about it, and my conversations with rockstar mentors produced countless stories.

My second thought was the list closely resembles the list of things to do to become a great leader. A terrific leader models admirable behavior. A mentoring relationship can do the same. Suppose a mentor gets a little selfish and focuses on herself and sets goals to improve in the areas I mentioned. In that case, she would become a better leader, and her mentee would see a leader who prioritized professional and personal development—up close and personal.

YOUR TURN TO TAKE A SELFISH

Over the years, as I grew as a mentor, I started to put my oxygen mask on first, but only when necessary. It finally sunk in through an unlikely illustration for learning and through a medium I generally avoid—television.

I watched *Schitt's Creek*, the award-winning Canadian show from its first season. In one of the earliest episodes, David Rose whines, "It's my turn to take a selfish." That now-famous line made me think about selfish mentoring for the first time.

For anyone who isn't a *Schitt's Creek* fan, David comments to his sister, Alexis, after telling him she wants to go out while David stays home (the rundown Rosebud Motel) to keep their needy parents' company. The phrase is now widely used when people believe they deserve something they want. What if, rather than a mentor experiencing fluky learning in mentoring partnerships, we strategically engineered it that way? We, as mentors, take a mentoring selfish.

Most people think mentoring is an act of giving; the mentor gives their time, advice, experience, and access. We may not consider other benefits to the mentor other than feeling good. As I talk to mentors, I think the relationship should be far more give and take, and perhaps the mentor should lean into receiving from their first interaction.

What if mentors practiced as we preached as Joan suggested. If we took the guidance we share with our mentoring partners and applied it to ourselves. Could we take the lead on our career development and lifetime learning as part of our mentoring? Do we strive to make all relationships opportunities for mutual learning? Do we assemble our "personal board of directors" that includes mentees as advisors? What if we actively sought out diverse mentees not just as part of a DEI or social justice initiative, but because we have much to learn?

Good mentors become great mentors not by focusing on their mentees, but by focusing on themselves, by taking a mentoring selfish. Many mentoring discussions involve the mentor doing most of the talking. I once received advice from a coaching coach that I should speak 85 percent of the time. I didn't hire him. I think we should strive to listen 85 percent of the time. We all like to talk about ourselves and our experiences. What if mentors paid more attention, talked less, and ultimately gave their mentees a lot more? Actions often speak louder than words; perhaps the best thing you can do as a leader/mentor is to be quiet. You allow your mentee to answer her question, boost her confidence, and you have time to think more deeply.

I've learned the hard way the only person I can control is myself. What if I did, rather than encouraging the mentee to take the lead in our partnership? With the focus on me, the mentor? Rather than navigating from the passenger seat while the mentee steers, the mentor and mentee both steer and navigate.

At some point, I had become a pretty good mentor, or so I'm told; I'd certainly had enough mentees both in formal programs and informal. Most of my mentees—some former—were thriving. Many earned promotions or found bigger jobs. They were happy in their professional and personal lives. I basked in a constant "mentoring glow" and had learned a bit from my mentees. I spoke at conferences. My quotes were online.

In addition to actual mentoring, I interviewed hundreds of mentees and mentors. Some interviews were part of the matching process, and others were to determine how the partnership was going. Veteran mentors often say, "I learned a lot from my mentee" or "I'm a better leader due to my mentoring experience." I realized I had learned from my partners as well. Wasn't that great? We had the mutual learning we sought. It was a great marketing blurb, but it was happening somewhat serendipitously.

My colleagues and I—all but one were volunteers—had designed and implemented a hugely successful global mentoring program that matched and supported hundreds of mentoring partnerships every year. We boasted our program was "mentee driven." We were obsessed with 50 percent of our participants, the mentees. We tracked the progress of our mentees and celebrated their achievements; one of our goals was to have a better representation of women in senior roles. We didn't think much about the mentors.

Leadership books recommend finding a mentor, and most professionals I know either have a mentor, or a few, or want one. Most mentors are more than happy to mentor but some are either over-committed with mentoring or find mentoring drains their energy when dealing with mentoring burnout. Mentors from underrepresented groups are in high demand with mentees of all backgrounds. In basic economic terms, the demand greatly exceeds the supply. The demand will naturally continue to increase as new mentees join the workforce. We need to find a way to increase the "supply" of mentors.

While mentoring can be a selfless endeavor, I'd encourage mentors to consider "taking a selfish" regularly for their benefit and that of their mentees. Whether you are a mentor or a mentee, you are primarily responsible for your growth and development. Why not take every opportunity to learn? Among other things, it's a great way to model the behavior you'd like to see in your mentee. Perhaps "selfish" is too strong of a word, and it might make you uncomfortable, but remember the advice you get every time you get on a plane and "put your oxygen mask on first." You cannot fill your mentee's cup from an empty well. Focus on yourself first. Be selfish, and your mentee will benefit. It's a mentoring win-win!

CHAPTER 8

CAREER ADVANCEMENT

"You can't just sit there and wait for people to give you that golden dream. You've got to get out there and make it happen for yourself."

DIANA ROSS

A LinkedIn report, "2021 Workplace Report," indicates 94 percent of employees would stay longer at a company if offered opportunities to learn and grow. Mentoring provides such opportunities, making a case for company-sponsored mentoring programs. A CNBC Workplace Happiness Survey reports, "Mentorship has an outsize impact on a worker's career across several measures."

Here are some highlight statistics:

- 71 percent of employees with a mentor say their company provides them with excellent or good opportunities to advance their careers.
- Just 47 percent of those without a mentor say the same.
- 89 percent of the mentees go on to mentor (my favorite statistic).

Mentoring is a powerful tool for career development and advancement; most mentees report career advancement as a goal. Additionally, mentoring can support both mentees and mentors in career transitions, whether voluntary or involuntary. In career advancement or change, mentors can help mentees imagine alternatives that the mentee may have never considered.

I caught up with my former colleague, Alka Banerjee, CEO of Emerging Ideas Inc. We reconnected when she commented on my LinkedIn post about mentoring. I recalled she had been one of our "go-to mentors." I didn't remember the best part of her mentoring story. Among the things I didn't recall was she started in our program as a mentee. "I was in the first phase," she explained.

She went on to tell me she joined the program after moving to New York from India and "wanted a mentor who understood how things worked in the United States. You matched me with Annie': she was perfect!"

She didn't have to share the last name; I replied, "Annie Shaeffer?" Annie was another serial mentor.

"Yes, Annie Shaeffer!" Alka went on to rave about their great partnership, "Annie was able to help [her] navigate a culture at a new company and in a new country." Alka is part of the 89 percent of mentees who go on to mentor and wanted to "pay it forward." by mentoring a non-US-based mentee who desired a connection to corporate headquarters. Alka was concerned when the implementation team matched her with a woman in Germany. Alka admitted, "I played into the stereotype Germans were rigid." She found her mentee was very prepared for every meeting and sent a thoughtful agenda before each phone call. "The agenda clearly outlined her goals, making it easy to focus on her goals and track progress." That organization served as an excellent foundation for a productive mentoring relationship.

There are many aspects to career advancement, such as moves into or between leadership positions. I'll focus on a few I've heard from many mentees:

STRATEGIC THINKING

As we move into leadership positions, we often shift from tactical action, which is specific and short-term, to strategic thinking. Strategic thinking involves the overall plan to support an organization's vision, and mission, and focuses on the future. The tactical plan is the actions taken to achieve the overall strategy. We go from being the person who does the work to the leader who decides what work gets done. I'm working with a mentee who has made the shift but is still getting feedback she's too tactical, which may be a communication issue (see the next section).

A former boss told me the easiest way to look at strategy is to think up, out, and forward. Mentors can support their partners by asking strategic questions themselves. What's next for you or your organization? What do you have to do to get there? What's going on in your industry/function? What's your vision and purpose, both as an individual and an organization? Another leader told me the best way to look like a strategic thinker is to ask strategic (rather than tactical) questions.

COMMUNICATION SKILLS

Mentors and mentees have an excellent opportunity to work on their communication skills in their partnership and to provide ongoing feedback. When we strive to be efficient, concise, and quick in our response, we often lose something. I've repeatedly banged out a short, immediate reaction to a text, then followed up with a "clarifying" text that wasn't much clearer. Sometimes it isn't clear who even sent the text. How often have you received a random text message, and your first question is "who is this?" The sender assumes you know who they are, but they aren't on your contact list.

It's appropriate for partners to discuss preferred methods of communication and boundaries.

I am a true New Yorker, and some (many) say I speak too quickly; a mentee (whose first language was Spanish) provided me feedback on my speed-talking years ago, and I will always be thankful to her. One of the most important lessons in communication is you need to meet the other person's needs.

Several years ago, I was a bit frustrated with my ability to communicate with my boss's boss in written form; we did just fine in person, in meetings, and on the phone, but something wasn't right when I sent e-mail updates.

I mentioned this to a mentee who knew the boss. He asked how I was communicating with the boss—great question—and told him I usually sent well-thought-out detailed updates. My mentee's response was perfect: "Michelle, he speaks PowerPoint." I started sending short presentations, and life was much better.

EXECUTIVE PRESENCE

Executive presence has become more challenging in our new virtual world with employees working from home and sometimes wearing sweats. I believe the classic advice "dress for the job you want, not the job you have" still applies. This guidance no longer means a navy suit and white shirt for most of us. Many businesses have moved to business casual or just plain casual, especially start-ups and specific industries. Still, you want to pay attention to how your boss and peers dress and how they present themselves.

It's not always fair, but people (think potential hiring managers and recruiters) will judge you on your appearance and for aspects of your appearance that have *nothing* to do with your performance. I've received feedback on my "unprofessional" (a.k.a. wild and curly) hair and chipped nail polish (it apparently indicated I was not conscientious).

Another thought for mentors: perhaps this is the ideal place to lead by example. You may have a great relationship with your partner, but this is primarily a professional relationship. Do you look like a leader? Are you willing to provide your mentee feedback when she doesn't show up appropriately?

COLLABORATION/TEAM BUILDING

Team skills are critical in positioning a mentee for career advancement. Often, a mentee has been an individual contributor, has supervised a person or two, or has interacted primarily with people in her department or group. Team is a critical component in leadership, and many managers consider it a "must-have." I've always thought this was a bit of a catch-22, you need the skill/experience to get the job, but you can't get the skill/experience without the job.

We certainly don't want to make things up. A great mentor can help her mentee explore or seek out opportunities to obtain team/collaboration experiences. Perhaps it's a special project or a volunteer position. I saw this with group mentoring, where each member co-facilitated sessions for the group. With the successful launch of our one-on-one mentoring program and expansion to include all Americas and Europe, we were anxious to diversify our "mentoring menu."

Once again, we turned to our partners at Menttium and our mentoring hero, Sue Stanek, and launched mentoring circles. These circles include a group of mentees (generally eight to twelve) with a mentor or two. There was no "matching" per se. The mentees were of similar stature in the organization, drawn from our employee resource groups, and all in-person (tied to a location). Not only did the circles permit better mentor/mentee ratios (at least from the perspective of the program organizers), but they provided an excellent opportunity for peer-to-peer learning and networking across business units.

I loved the concept but was disappointed I couldn't participate in the circles as a mentor as my travel schedule would not permit it. The circles met in person, and I was frequently out of the office, and it wasn't uncommon to have a last-minute meeting hit my calendar. I wanted to share the experience and was hopeful that I would find a way to participate. I believed I could better lead the program if I had first-hand experience. One group gave me that opportunity.

Each circle mapped out their learning objectives at the first meeting, and members rotated co-facilitating the sessions with the mentor's support. Elevator pitches were a common topic, and this team developed a plan to achieve that learning objective and add in some networking (another common subject).

Each member drafted her elevator pitch, which the members reviewed as a group. The next step was to practice with each other. Then they hit pay dirt! Each circle member—including the mentors—invited a senior leader to join a lunch networking event. Such a brilliant approach! Some circle members had never been in the room with our senior executives unless it was an event like a company town hall or annual meeting.

My first stroke of luck was that Laurie Meisel—the social media guru who introduced me to LinkedIn—invited me. The next was when mentor Connie Bennett—one of the women leading our WINS program and a senior sales leader who spent most of her career with Business Week— invited Glenn Goldberg. Glenn was the president of McGraw Hill's Information and Media Group, a repeat mentor, and an all-around nice guy.

The circle started the session on their own; I joined as a special (at least in my eyes) guest as they practiced their elevator speeches with each other. Several women shared they hated networking; I admitted I didn't love it either but it was one of those things you had to do, like going to the dentist. This revelation surprised many people; they'd seen me speaking in front of large rooms with hundreds of people. As an introvert, walking up to a "stranger" and introducing myself is way out of my comfort zone.

I like to be over-prepared for mostly everything and had spent some time thinking about what I would say during my remarks that day. But the ladies threw me a curveball. I was thrilled to listen to their elevator pitches and provide feedback. Everything was great until someone asked, "What about you, Michelle?"

"What about me? You know who I am," I replied, ready to move on.

That wasn't happening. Another member chimed in, "Do your elevator pitch." The only thing I like less than networking was talking about myself...and elevator pitches, but I was supposedly the leader of this group.

I launched into my acronym-filled "pitch." "I'm Michelle Ferguson. I'm the SVP of Finance for the HPI (Higher Education, Professional, and International) Group at MHE (McGraw Hill Education). I'm the proud founder and self-proclaimed "mother" of WINS and a co-founder of the mentoring program." A short elevator ride indeed.

There was a pregnant pause, they looked at each other, and someone finally got brave enough to say, "Is that all you've got? You're better than that." I was. The group knew who I was, but I was undoubtedly in rooms with people who didn't, and my elevator pitch was awful. I now work on it regularly.

This story illustrates the beauty of mentoring; everyone involved learned something. Two of the mentees developed facilitating/teaching skills and all of the mentees honed their elevator pitches and learned to network. The senior executives knew more about what was happening on the ground floor. I realized I needed a great elevator pitch and I could learn from mentees or almost anyone if I was open to it.

DEI

I've covered this in Chapter 6, but I believe it's worth a reminder. More and more organizations are committing to a more equitable and inclusive workplace and more diverse teams. Mentors can work with their mentees to ensure not just the right intentions concerning DEI but to ensure their mentee has a great story to tell...and she can articulate that story well. It's not enough to say, "I read a book" (I've heard that from senior executives). A leader must take action and actively support DEI efforts.

CAREER TRANSITIONS

I partnered with a mentee—let's call her Stevie—through a Menttium program. Before I met Stevie, I recall reviewing her profile and wondering, "What am I doing mentoring this woman?" We had similar titles, work experience, and were approximately the same age. Like me, Stevie had spent a good part of her career at the same company and had risen from an entry-level role to a senior vice president role. Her goal in joining a mentoring program (which her company sponsored and paid for) was to break into the C-suite—the very top level of leadership. I had a similar goal—and finally hit it.

For most of our year together, nothing remarkable transpired. We worked on improving Stevie's visibility in her organization. She was in the Midwest, and her boss—and most of his peers—were in New York. Late in the year, her boss called to tell her he was planning to visit her location, a first. We worked together to prep Stevie for the boss' visit, focusing on strategies to support her goal of a promotion. At this point, you may have figured out what comes next, but neither of us did. Let's say there was a wild card.

The day after the visit, Stevie requested an impromptu meeting with me. I suspected things had not gone as we had planned. That was an understatement; her boss had come to town to announce a reorganization that eliminated her position. She was understandably upset and confused. In less than a year, she went from preparing for her next step to out the door. After decades with the company. I understood completely.

We worked through the five stages of grief: the stages of grief and job loss are similar.

Denial – "I'm waiting for him to call back and tell me it was a mistake."

Anger – "How could they do it to me after twenty-five years with the company?"

Bargaining – "Do you think I should call him and ask him to reconsider? Maybe I can take a cut in pay..."

Depression – "I just want to hang with my dogs."

Acceptance. – "I want more free time to travel."

Stevie's husband was retiring, and her son lived out of state. They loved to travel to competitions with their dogs. Perhaps this was a blessing in disguise. She started exploring part-time roles in non-profits. She became a networking and LinkedIn genius.

Two months later, I called her to update her; my boss eliminated my new C-suite role. I saw it coming; maybe because her experience made me more aware. She supported me in working through the five stages, and her career pivot led me to pursue a pivot in my career.

Sometime after that, Stevie called to share she had landed a part-time chief operating officer role at a non-profit with a mission that moved her.

Career transitions can be difficult, whether voluntary or not. I'll tackle them separately as I believe there are nuanced differences between quitting your job voluntarily and losing your job.

VOLUNTARY CAREER TRANSITIONS

In 2019, I heard Kathryn Minshew, a founder of The Muse, speak at Chief, a private women's network focused on connecting and supporting women executive leaders (I'm a proud founding member). When asked, "What's your biggest weakness?" she quickly replied, "I'm too persistent."

The answer struck me, as I'd always struggled with answering that question, and I realized persistence was often my biggest weakness. I'm like a dog with a bone—I won't let go. I've found many of my mentees and others struggle with excessive persistence. Many people stay in suboptimal roles because leaving without another job seems risky or irresponsible. Leaving a job involves risk, and many of us are risk-averse. PokerDivas founder and CEO Ellen Leikind believes the strategic risk-taking skills she's developed as a recreational poker player have transferred to business and career decisions.

Mentees often seek a mentor (or are matched with one) as they want to do more, and sometimes that desire to do more grows out of frustration with where they are. The boss might not be great; values are misaligned, opportunities for growth/learning are limited, or she is just plain burned out. Can the current role be changed to better suit her needs? Can she find a side hustle within the organization or outside that can help fuel her passions? Are there opportunities within the broader organization? For me, that came in starting a women's initiative and co-founding a mentoring program at McGraw Hill-S&P Global.

Here's a story about an unlikely career transition:

I worked with a mentee, let's call her Joy, who was a project manager and felt stuck in her current organization. At the time, her global company was launching a six-sigma initiative. I knew there was a role in human resources that might be interesting for her. Joy was less than interested and thought perhaps it was time to look elsewhere. I persisted and suggested at a minimum, she would get her Six Sigma black belt, which was a plus for a project manager. Six Sigma is a set of tools and techniques for process improvement. The hiring manager was a great guy. Joy took the interview and the job. Where is she now? She is a talent manager leader—with a black belt.

Sometimes, a mentee's existing role or organization is no longer a great fit, and it's time to fold 'em (poker reference). A mentor can help her mentee make the big decision: Do I start looking for a job while I am still working? Or do I resign without a role so I can catch my breath and work on the job search full-time? I see this happening more often and admire people who make this bold move.

In the *Pursuing Perfect* podcast, certified professional coach Marissa Fernandez talks about the signs you are ready for a career transition. Some questions Marissa suggests you ask your mentee and perhaps yourself are:

- What does career success and fulfillment look like for me, beyond money and title? Am I on the path toward that vision?
- In my current job, am I using my greatest strengths?
- At the end of the day, do I have the energy for my life and passions outside of work, or am I completely drained? (We'll dive into this in the work-life chapter.)
- Do my company's values align with my own?
- Am I proud of my work?
- Do I have people to support, encourage, and inspire me?
- When I look at my boss's job and his/her boss's job, is that something that inspires me?

The answers to those questions will provide a mentee with clarity on "do I stay or do I go?"

INVOLUNTARY CAREER TRANSITION

Losing your job is not fun regardless of the situation, whether as part of a reorganization or for some apparent cause. Most of us don't have the luxury—or desire—to wallow in our grief for long. I believe you need to take some time to grieve and heal.

The involuntary timeout is a perfect time to reassess your career. A mentor can help clarify what you want in a role or organization. Do you want to change fields/

industries? Perhaps work less than full-time (or move to full-time)? Work from an office, remotely, or in a hybrid environment? Many women I know turn a termination into the opportunity to do something independently. Perhaps even better, job transition is a perfect opportunity to join a mentoring (or similar) cohort to share information, best practices, leads, and support.

Career transition is an ideal time for a mentor to open up her network, as networking is perhaps the most productive strategy for a job search. According to HubSpot, 85 percent of job seekers find a job through networking, and CNBC reports 70 percent of jobs are never published publicly (the infamous "hidden" job market).

I reached out to one of my former mentees to get some general inspiration for this book. Let's call her Anna. We started as usual with a personal catch-up: how are the kids and dogs? How are things in Chicago? And then we got to work.

Our timing was perfect. Anna's boss had scheduled an "update" Zoom with her and her team for the day before. Most of the team have always worked remotely, and they have always done virtual team meetings. The company and group are in an industry kept very busy during the pandemic and have seen increased turnover (not unusual for the industry). They are finally at full employment, and their heavy workload continues.

Anna and her team were hoping for some help; that's not what they got. Instead, the boss shared the budget:

revenues were down (they have nothing to do with income) and went one step further and compared their budget to the budget of another group—which was doing better from a financial perspective. His message was the team needed to work even harder, that any future openings would likely be unfilled.

Anna now has multiple problems: her team is demoralized, and she needs to help them remain productive and engaged. Her boss hadn't given her any warning on the meeting subject, and she had not previously seen the budget. While this particular prank was a first, it was consistent with his pattern of behavior.

The boss had little concern with her advancement—it could be because he didn't want to lose her—but she doesn't know that for sure. Anna's been at this company for more than a decade. She finished her story, and rather than asking a question (the right thing to do), I said, "You know what you have to do." She responded that she did, and we started to work on a transition strategy. She's out of practice as she hasn't looked for a job in over a decade, and I shared some resources.

Author Kim Scott told me a story of approaching her mentor, Sheryl Sandberg, who was at Google at the time, about a potential role at another organization. After some exploration, Sheryl suggested, "Why don't you come work for me?" I haven't seen many similar examples, but mentors I know have encouraged their partners to explore options outside their comfort zone and way off their career paths.

One final thought and a reminder on mentoring and career advancement. As discussed in Chapter 1, mentoring is not sponsorship and is usually *not* directly tied to advancement. I've heard of a few corporate programs—often focused on underrepresented groups—that include mentoring as part of a program aimed specifically at promotions for participants. While mentors can support mentees in their quest for career advancement by identifying skills and strategies and opening their virtual black book, there is no guarantee or even a promotion commitment.

Mentoring is mentoring. It can support both partners in their career advancement and support partners in career transitions.

CHAPTER 9

WORK-LIFE BLENDING

"You can have it all. Just not all at once."

OPRAH WINFREY

"Most of us have trouble juggling. The woman who says she doesn't is someone whom I admire but have never met."

BARBARA WALTERS

No, it's not a typo in the chapter title—I meant to say blending, not balance. I never understood the Themis (Lady Justice) scales metaphor. Or perhaps the problem was my scales have always been off balance. It's not that when I walked out of the office, I left "work" behind, and after my commute, life resumed. Being in the office didn't mean the school nurse couldn't call or my father or sons wouldn't end up in the ER...or there would be enough food at home for the kids and the dogs. Conversely, I don't remember when I wasn't doing calls or working from home. So, I prefer to strive toward blending or integrating the two.

Jaime Ellis and I are writing partners and supported each other as we wrote our books. We've had a few writing dates along the way, and she has shared one of her coaches advised she should write the book she most needs to read *now*. I'm not sure I wrote the book I most needed at the time, but this is undoubtedly the chapter I most needed. I am on the road to getting better at blending work and life, but I have lots of work to do. Of all the lessons I've taught and learned, this was the hardest and took the longest to figure out.

This section might be a great "mentoring moment" for me...since I'm not so great at work-life blending. This work is ongoing and requires adjusting as new responsibilities add to your life. I did! And it might be another lesson for mentors; you don't know everything. You can admit that to your partner.

We are not alone. I interviewed many people for this book; given the subject, the interviewees were primarily women. The women had many great stories to share about mentoring and the mentoring topics covered in the book. Positive stories about work-life blending were hard to find.

A September 2021 article in Mental Health UK.org says, "It's not so much about splitting your time fifty-fifty between work and leisure, but making sure you feel fulfilled in both areas of your life."

"Work-Life Balance Is A Cycle; Not an Achievement" is a *Harvard Business Review* article. The authors say, "Despite the resounding evidence working long hours can be harmful to both employees and employers, many professionals struggle to overcome their assumptions they must work long hours to succeed—and their deeply ingrained habits—around work hours."

The work-life cycle includes five distinct steps:

1. Pause and denormalize - Take a breath and remind yourself working around the clock is not normal or healthy.
2. Pay attention to your emotions - How are you feeling? Guilty? Overwhelmed? Frustrated?
3. Reprioritize - What do you have a lot on your plate? What's essential, and what can be delegated, deferred, or not done?
4. Consider your alternatives.
5. Implement changes.

Overall, mentoring provides an opportunity to pause and focus on your emotions. Frameworks like this are helpful in discussions with your mentoring partner and reflecting on yourself. Here's an example of the steps in a real-life mentoring situation where a woman finds herself on e-mails until almost midnight.

1. Pause and remind yourself (or your partner) this is not normal. Are your colleagues responding at midnight? Is everyone else sleeping?
2. How does it make you feel? Put actual words to the emotion and share with your partner.
3. Consider what you are doing during the typical workday that causes the need for late-night e-mails. Too

many meetings? Excessive cc-ing on e-mails? No designated time for administrative tasks? Do you have FOMO and insist on reading and responding to all e-mails? Does some part of you think it makes you look good?

4. What else can you do? Tell your colleagues you are not available for e-mails after dinner? Hide your laptop in the closet (I've done it)? Join a yoga class that meets in the evening? Create time in your nine-to-five schedule to respond to e-mails?

5. Do something! Start with one thing. Perhaps find a partner to hold you accountable.

Since I believe work-life is an ideal opportunity for both mentees and mentors to grow, I thought I'd speak to someone who was both a mentor and a mentee. Sudeshna Sen is a vice president of marketing at Merkle, a DEI leader, a board member, and an all-around Wonder Woman. She shared the best advice she ever received was from a mentor who is now a CEO.

His advice was, "As you move up the ladder, always remember your values." She added, "Nothing is black and white anymore, and your values will define how you take your next action."

It took me a little time to figure out how that tied into work-life, but I had an "aha" moment as I noodled it. I realized while I had never received that advice regarding work-life balance, I was accidentally living it.

In late 2019, I attended a presentation on core personal values. It includes a three-step process:

1. Define your core personal values.
2. Structure your life around what you have defined.
3. Ensure everything aligns with them.

It's challenging to align everything with values; I can't directly tie cleaning my bathroom to my values. The exercise of defining my core personal values and writing them down on a now tea-stained index card helps me prioritize every day, week, and month.

I realized when I face some work-life decisions—like watching my grandkids, working on my book, catching up on e-mails, or taking a long walk by the river—just looking at the card helps me answer the question. As I thought about it, I realized never have I ever heard someone define their core personal values as anything like "work more hours," "empty e-mail inbox," or "finish/edit a presentation." The acts of defining your top three or four values and writing them down help you prioritize; when you face a decision on whether to go to the gym or answer e-mails, looking at your core values list, which includes "health," will help with priorities.

Setting boundaries can support living your life in alignment with your values. For example, if the family is a core value, you may decide that family dinner is a priority. You can set boundaries by blocking the time on your calendar and leaving your phone in another room. You could share boundaries with your colleagues and tell them you will not take calls or respond to e-mails or texts during dinner hours.

Back to my work-life conversation with Sudeshna. We moved on to her advice as a mentor and leader. She thought work-life blending was mainly about setting boundaries. In addition to her role as vice president of marketing, she co-leads a DEI program. Here's her take on mentoring and work-life: "Work-life is one of the most critical topics I've run into with why mentees...especially those with small kids. Both parents are struggling with work-life balance...especially in the pandemic."

Her advice is to "define some boundaries and share them." Setting boundaries isn't all that hard, and communicating isn't that hard either. It seems to me the challenge is sticking to them. Sudeshna's advice is "just do it" for women in particular; the guys do. Sudeshna adds, "When they (men) work from home, they will block time to eat, maybe even make lunch or eat lunch with their kids. And they are unapologetic about it." I've started peeking into the gym in my apartment building in New York during the workday. I don't know the gender split of the building residents, but given over one thousand residents, I guess it's close to fifty-fifty. Who do I see in the gym between nine and five? Primarily men, primarily "working" age (i.e., not fifteen and not eighty-five). It appears men are more willing to take time during the business day to exercise than women are...at least in my building.

Sudeshna suggests "mentors and leaders need to model the behavior." They need to lead by example. If you choose to send e-mails in the evening after you eat dinner/get the kids to bed/feed the cat, be *very* clear you are doing it because it's convenient for you. And be *very* clear you do not expect responses "off hours."

You can even use a scheduling app/software. These apps help avoid time zone challenges, find the best times for the recipient(s), and show you are thoughtful. You write the e-mail now and schedule delivery appropriately for the other person.

Suppose you are on the receiving end of the off-hours e-mail/slack/text. The sender may be oblivious or in another time zone. Your initial response may be to reply immediately. Take a breath. Did the sender say or imply in any way it was urgent? Or is that an assumption on your part?

While the focus of this book is women mentoring women, I don't believe work-life blending is an issue for just women or working moms. Work-life blending is critical for a healthy work environment and can reduce stress and burnout.

As I was writing this chapter, I realized I still hadn't done this topic justice, and I thought, "Who do I know who has this nailed?" The answer was Marissa Fernandez, a certified professional coach, performance strategist, and former chief marketing officer. Not only did Marissa agree to speak to me—she sent an outline in advance. Here's the outline and some notes from our conversation:

- Define what "balance" looks like for you.

As mentioned in the article in MentalHealth UK earlier in this chapter, "balance" might not mean fifty-fifty. It might mean working like a demon from 7 a.m. to 5 p.m. and then going out for a run. It might mean taking two hours midday to work out and eat lunch. The challenging part here is you need to define it for yourself. No one else's model will work.

- Create intention and systems to design the balance (life by design vs. default).

This point is essential for maintaining the balance you just defined. Marissa's excellent question is, "Are you designing your future, or are you living in the default future? That is what happens when you don't have plans and systems in place." The default future could look like you continue in your current role working full-time, perhaps get a promotion or two, live in the same place, travel to the same places with the same people, until you retire and take up golf. Marissa blocks an hour for lunch each day (so do I). She adds it may not seem like much, but it ensures you eat lunch and maintain your energy. For me, it also means the dogs get walked. She suggests you have to make sure you schedule "life"—"work has a way of creeping into every open space." Life, not so much.

- Decide what is essential. Connect not just to what it is, but *why* it is necessary.

This comment made me think of Stephen Covey's time management matrix (from his book *The 7 Habits of Highly Effective People*—published in 1989 but still relevant). The matrix is part of Habit 3: Put First Things First and divides activities into four quadrants, with "important" on one axis and "urgent" on the other. Covey defines importance as "has to do with results. If something is important, it contributes to your mission, your values, and your high priority goals." He urges readers to focus on the important rather than the urgent, as does Marissa, who adds the "why" question. I once heard someone suggest you include the "why" on every "to-do" item. Cleaning the bathroom may be easier to tackle if you frame it around maintaining your health and your family's health.

Marissa recommends making a list of what's important, which will help you identify what's not essential. It would be best to stop doing unimportant things (although it's not that simple).

- Time Management and Energy Management
Marissa notes many of her clients think they need to be better at managing their time but adds you need to learn to manage your energy. We all have the same twenty-four hours in the day, but you will be more productive if you do things that fuel your energy. Conversely, think about the things that drain your energy: maybe Zoom calls or endless e-mails. See if you can replace just fifteen minutes a day of energy-sucking activities with energy-enhancing activities.

- Everything in the calendar. Personal stuff.
"You have to be in the driver's seat of your calendar." If you leave your calendar to other people, it will become a reflection of other people's priorities. Marissa takes ninety minutes every Monday morning to plan out her week, including personal time. Schedule it rather than

putting "go for a run" on your to-do list. Whether work or personal, get it on your calendar if it's essential.

- To-Dos – Do / Ditch / Delay / Delegate / Downgrade. The "Dos" go *in the calendar.*

Marissa puts all of her "to do's" into five buckets:

1. Do – Pretty self-explanatory.
2. Ditch – Take it off the list and don't do it.
3. Delay – Can the item wait a day, a week, a month?
4. Delegate – Can this task be outsourced?
5. Downgrade – Many women are perfectionists. Some tasks require your "A" game...many do not. Does the e-mail need to be edited...again? My friend Sue Stanek says, "Sometimes good enough is good enough."
6. Communicate goals and boundaries.

"This one is about creating allies," Marissa explains. She suggests rating yourself on setting boundaries on a scale of one to ten (do it, please), and if you are anything but a ten, identify what it would take to get you one point higher on the scale. Say you're at seven and decide that getting away from your desk for sixty minutes at midday will move you to an eight. Here's the key: go one step further and tell your boss, partner, team, and anyone who will listen. Enlist allies! As a numbers gal, I like this suggestion. It's something tangible and actionable.

- Leaders: lead by example. Understand how the team defines balance. What's important to them? Offer flexibility.

As a leader or a mentor, you are not just doing this for yourself. It would help determine how individuals define balance and what it means for the team. Perhaps it's no scheduled meetings, including your mentoring meeting after 5:00 p.m., or no e-mails on the weekend. Or everyone gets an hour "out of office" each day...at a time that suits them.

In Chapter 6, I introduced Mariana Saddakni. She has an interesting approach to looking at the challenge of work-life blending. She is of Italian-Greek-Syrian-Lebanese heritage, raised in Argentina, and lives and works in New York City. Mariana has a husband and two school-aged, special needs kids and no family support in the United States. She explains, "It's very lucky we were raised in a culture of the 'we' is first, not achievement and not the money." Her cultural background helps her prioritize family. She adds, "Of course, we all like money!"

Mariana, a true innovator, developed a "minimum viable product" for her life early in her career. Most of us are familiar with this concept at work. A minimum viable product (MVP) is a product version with just enough features to be used by early customers who can then provide feedback for future product development. Perhaps even more relevant for this conversation, focusing on releasing an MVP means potentially avoiding lengthy and unnecessary work.

For Mariana and her husband, that meant living in NYC—in Midtown, which is not usually a preferred residential neighborhood—where both worked full-time and could walk to work. By living close to their offices, they could easily attend school events which were essential to them. She abandoned the thought of a white picket fence and a swimming pool and hasn't looked back.

They extended the MVP concept to their financial life as "[they] are both employees...so [they] have a fixed income". While both successful, they are realistic that "things happen and designing an MVP life that would allow the mortgage to get paid and the lights to stay on even if one of us wasn't working. That also reduced stress and energy drain." Their location also supports her work-life blending by allowing easy access to Central Park, where she loves to run. Mariana attributes some of her MVP mindset to her "immigrant mentality." She focuses on what's important to her; her family and financial security. She doesn't need to have it all.

Mariana's story makes me think of Marissa Fernandez's question on whether you are intentionally designing your life. Mariana certainly did.

Work-life blending is an area where it is imperative that a mentor lead by example. It isn't sincere to provide mentoring on work-life balance and schedule your mentoring sessions on Sunday mornings as you can't find time during the week. While I love doing mentoring calls on weekends when I tend to be distracted by work commitments, a mentee could perceive a Sunday morning call as a violation of her boundaries and an intrusion into her personal time.

I love the Barbara Walters' quote about juggling. We're all trying to keep lots of balls in the air; it's an ongoing struggle. Work-life blending is a common topic in mentoring conversations and an opportunity for growth for both partners.

CHAPTER 10

GENDER PAY GAP

*"This isn't about a money grab. It's about doing the fair thing.
It's about treating people the way they deserve to be treated,
no matter their gender."*

CARLI LLOYD

A woman in a mentoring cohort I'm involved with received a job offer for a role that seemed to be a perfect fit. Unfortunately, the compensation and the title didn't fit so well. The salary was well below what she had been making, and the title was vice president rather than senior vice president. The offer was insulting—to her, the cohort, and women overall.

The group strategized, researched, and suggested she ask for a senior vice president title and 25 percent more base salary. She had data on comparable positions—compensation, title, and responsibilities. She watched a Cindy Gallop video to get her ready for battle! The group prepared her for the inevitable pushback and questions.

She made her proposal to her new boss, who responded, "You're right. Let me talk to HR."

Much mentoring guidance suggests the partnership should be mentee-driven with a focus on the developmental needs of the mentee. For years, my goal was to stay true to that guidance. Still, I now realize there is one area in which a great mentor, particularly of women, needs to take the bull by the horns (a terrible metaphor for a book primarily about women), which is gender pay equity.

Most women—and some men—can relate to this story. I was recruited for a role early in my career by a male senior executive. The hiring manager (who mainly was my boss on paper—but that's another story) was a woman; everyone else I spoke to during the hiring process was a white male, as was the incumbent in the role. At the time, I thought nothing of it.

I received an offer and accepted it—without negotiation or any actual research on the job market. The job title was controller—a technical role. As part of my new role I had access to the numbers, including salary.

I was curious as to the compensation of my team; compensation was the most significant component of our budget. My initial finding was odd; I had two direct reports who were director-level. The woman was seemingly better qualified, as she had a degree in accounting, than her male counterpart, who had no degree in a director of finance and accounting role. He was at a higher-grade level and made approximately 20 percent more money! There was a "gap" between a man and a woman with similar titles, experience, and responsibilities.

Well, that wasn't good. I expanded my review and found the salary details on my predecessor. Again, on paper, I had better credentials, a degree in accounting, and a CPA—as a reminder, this was a controller role—the top accountant in the department. Bob had a degree in something other than accounting and wasn't a CPA. I would later learn that his accounting knowledge was dated. The real problem was I was at a lower "level," as most large organizations have pay bands, with the same responsibility. My salary was lower. I was ineligible for a not-insignificant bonus. My personal "gap" was well more than 25 percent. Again, there was a gap between the compensation of two people in the same role.

I'm embarrassed to say I did nothing—about either gap—at the time.

A woman in my network handled a similar situation much better than I did. She had just moved into a people manager role in a large tech company (you would recognize the name). In her first review of the salaries for her team, she realized "some of the women in her group were making less than their male counterparts despite having the more relevant experience." She consulted with her mentor, and they mapped out a presentation with the details of this gender gap which she presented to her boss—she focused on the facts.

This leader corrected pay inequities and did the right thing. She also reduced the reputational and financial risk for her organization had the injustices surfaced in another way. Not only did her manager acknowledge the problem, but they corrected the inequity and prompted the overall organization to perform a review that revealed other pay inequality.

That was some time ago, and unfortunately, my story wasn't unique. The gender pay gap is still unacceptable. The gender pay gap narrowed slightly but has remained constant for the past fifteen years. We won't have parity at the rate we are going until 2059. A Pew Research study reports women still make 84 percent of what men earn on average. The same report indicates the news is better for younger women; women in the twenty-five to thirty-four age range make up 93 percent of their male counterparts on average.

The stats for non-white women are even poorer. A study by LeanIn reports, on average, Black women in the US earn 37 percent less than white men and 20 percent less than white women. It's even worse for educated Black women. The statistics for other women of color are equally disturbing. Some estimates are women can lose five hundred thousand dollars in compensation over their careers, and the impact on Black women may be twice that.

In a 2021 interview with Chief, the network for professional women, Gloria Steinem, the feminist, journalist, and social-political activist said the number-one priority for feminists is creating gender pay equity. Most feminist activists agree. Who will disagree with Gloria?

I spoke to Jane Lacher, a futurist, strategist, and enthusiastic advocate for women, who shares this belief. She went on to say there were three critical components for women in our quest to reduce the gender pay gap: 1) find a sponsor, 2) network effectively, and 3) find a mentor.

Concerning mentoring, Jane suggests mentors can support their mentees in becoming more comfortable with compensation negotiation. Compensation is an area where a mentor in the same field may have access to better compensation data or access people in her network with that data. As mentors, we can start by having salary conversations with our mentees; share your information and any other information. Normalize these conversations.

A 2020 McKinsey & Co. report indicated the representation of women in senior vice president levels grew from 23 percent to 28 percent from January 2015 to January 2020, and the representation of women in C-suite roles grew from 17 percent to 21 percent. Still, women make up more than 50 percent of the workforce. Mentors can encourage their mentees to pursue more senior roles. Jane also suggests mentoring can also help "right-size" the representation of women in senior positions.

Salary negotiations for women can be a double-edged sword—are we too friendly or assertive/aggressive? Most of the women I know received guidance to be "nice girls" and selfless. That has cost us in many ways, especially when it comes to compensation—and it starts early when women first joined the workforce. A one-thousand-dollar difference in starting salary results in a 1,344-dollar differential in ten years (assuming 3 percent interest compounded annually). A third higher in just ten years!

Mentoring college and university students or other first-time job seekers can reduce the inequality in starting salaries. Mentors can help mentees gather data and then roleplay a salary negotiation.

Mentors, especially women mentors, need to counsel and support their mentees in salary negotiations. Cindy Gallop, a diversity consultant, and speaker suggests in a talk at Chief that women "ask for the largest number you can say out loud without laughing" and women should "learn to think like straight white men."

Mentors should empower their partners to advocate for themselves and ask for more. They can support their mentee in researching compensation information, sharing their compensation data and strategies, and enlisting their network to help the mentee.

One of my writing partners, Sandhya Jain-Patel, circulates a spreadsheet on compensation for executive women; you provide your data to gain access. You can check job postings; certain states now require posted open positions include salary ranges.

Mentors should guide their mentees in the annual review and salary increase process—and perhaps lead by example in properly preparing themselves. I've heard countless women express concerns they will sound "arrogant" if they talk about their accomplishments. A good mentor will reassure her mentee to take personality out of it and stick to the facts around achievements. A pay equity expert said the key was to "document the value of your role."

Many companies have seemingly strict guidelines for salary increases, with a "pool" of money spread among all employees. This limitation may make salary discussions especially tough for some women. "If I get more, someone else gets less." A mentor can help the mentee focus on herself rather than the group and ensure she gets her fair share of the compensation pie. The mentor can also support the mentee in pursuing "workarounds" to salary increase limitations. Is there a potential for a salary review every six months rather than annually? Is there an option for bonuses? Or additional PTO (personal time off) or a more flexible schedule? Reimbursement for training or memberships? Equity?

Here's an example. Many organizations have formal compensation and incentive plans with performance targets. Mine did, and I had a formal plan that included personal and company-wide targets (part of the bonus was based on our financial performance). I co-led a large project which, I assumed it would help the personal performance part of my annual bonus. I didn't ask for a bonus for the project's successful completion, which had a significant positive financial impact on the company. My male co-lead asked for an additional bonus...and got it.

A spot bonus is paid "on the spot" to an individual, team, or even the entire organization. The payment is often for a specific project or result. While they tend to be small (less than an annual bonus), unless there is a particular goal (e.g., each team member earns one thousand dollars when the project is on time), they can be discretionary. Some employees may not know about them, so they never ask for a spot or discretionary bonus.

Maria Colacurcio, a leading pay equity expert and CEO of Syndio, refers to these "workarounds" as "the dirty little secrets of compensation" in a Chief event. She shared a story of a friend who was surprised when a colleague received a spot bonus; she was unaware that such a thing existed.

A mentee can ask the simple question, "why am I paid what I'm paid?" and move on to "How can I move up? What skills and experiences do I need to receive a promotion?"

A mentor can support her mentee at a broader pay equity level by suggesting the mentee ask her manager or human resources if the company does pay equity reviews. Does the company share or plan to share the results? If not, what's the rationale.

Compensation negotiations are the perfect place to share your experiences—good and bad. I've already shared a story of where I failed to advocate for myself or my team. A much better story was the guidance I received from a colleague in Human Resources. I was fretting about my annual increase. There was a three percent "pool" that year, and I felt I had a great year with facts to support it. So, I should get something more, maybe four percent.

His response was eye-opening for me. "Really, Michelle? You are worried about a one percent difference in your increase?" He suggested I focus on my bonus; that potential was huge. What if I could get ten percent more in my bonus? Or more stock? Both of those options were worth more than one percent of my salary. I guess Bob was a "drive-by mentor"—even if neither of us knew it at the time.

The gender pay gap has been an issue for some time, and like many other things, the pandemic has highlighted the problems.

We've already discussed COVID, its impact on women, and mentoring in Chapter 5. Our "new" normal creates challenges concerning compensation and the gender pay gap. Remote and hybrid work have become more common, and women tend to take greater advantage of these options for various reasons, including childcare. This shift to remote/virtual work may seem like a big win for women, but can lead to unintended implications. Inequity in pay can result from additional challenges such as "proximity bias." Proximity bias boils down to getting the good/new assignments—and the corresponding increase in pay and promotions because you are the person physically closest to the boss.

A great mentor can work with her mentee to develop strategies to improve her non-physical presence to offset the proximity bias. Perhaps you volunteer for assignments or send daily text updates to your boss. It's the modern-day "out of sight, out of mind" challenge, and remote workers have dealt with it for years.

Let's return to the Chief session with Gloria Steinem. While she believes we need better laws to reduce the gender pay gap, like reforms that make it illegal to ask about current and past salary, Gloria believes "some of it is internal." We as women especially tend to measure ourselves against the ideal of the person who occupies the job." She says, "Don't measure yourself against the ideal; measure yourself against Harry who now has the job. It's a totally different standard."

This guidance can form the basis for a tremendous mentoring conversation, especially for perfectionist women. A finding in LinkedIn's "The Perfection Trap" says the desire to be perfect—Gloria's "idea" —is one of the two most pressing costs that women face.

Perfectionism in women often starts in childhood, where girls receive stars for being obedient and good students. Schools tend to penalize girls more than boys for "aggressive" behavior when schools may overlook similar behavior in boys. Voltaire's famous quote seems to fit: "Perfect is the enemy of the good." Mentors can support their partners by focusing on good rather than perfect.

Alex Carter, author of *Ask for More* and a clinical professor of law and director of the Mediation Clinic at Columbia Law School, shared the story of seeking salary negotiation guidance from a mentor early in her career during a Zoom webinar. Her guidance was to negotiate hard "for the sisterhood" (her words). Your salary negotiation and your encouragement of your mentee to advocate and negotiate for herself will benefit her and help raise the bar for all women and reduce the unacceptable gender wage gap. We can't wait until 2059.

Perhaps the most significant value a mentor can provide her mentee in any negotiation is to discourage the mentee from being her own worst enemy. Often, the real "enemy" in negotiation is ourselves. The mentee prepares for the negotiation; she needs data and confidence. Frame the negotiation as a conversation between equals. Your mentee has plenty to offer.

And a final thought.

While women mentoring women can help reduce the gap, women mentoring men could also help bridge this gap. At a minimum, it would increase awareness and result in more willingness to see people as people and strive for the success of all people, regardless of gender, race, or ethnicity.

The gender pay gap is an issue for men and women. All genders can utilize mentoring to narrow the gap—perhaps even eliminate it before 2059!

CONCLUSION

"A mentor is not someone who walks ahead of us and tells us how they did it. A mentor is someone who walks alongside us to guide us on what we can do."

SIMON SINEK, AUTHOR

Mentoring is often cited as critical for the advancement of employees, especially when the goal is a leadership position. While mentoring has been around since the time of the Greeks, it's a very different business now—with more diverse players. The first mentor (Mentor) was a guy as was his mentee. More and more women are seeking mentors, and in many cases, they are seeking mentors who are also women.

The number of women in senior positions is slowly increasing, which means more senior women can serve as mentors. That's good news on many levels, but there are still challenges we all play a part in solving. In economic terms, we have problems with both supply, which is fewer men willing to mentor and mentors with more demands on their time, and demand, which is more women in the pipeline who want mentors and mentees who desire multiple mentors.

I am a mentoring zealot (moderation is not one of my strengths). I've had the good fortune to have dozens of mentoring partners, co-lead global mentoring programs with different formats (traditional one-on-one, mentoring circles, and reverse mentoring), and participate in mentoring cohorts. My initial motivation was altruistic—there was a need no one was filling. I had a passion and loved fixing things. I wanted to support advancing more women into leadership positions. I knew *nothing* about mentoring and had only participated in one formal program—with a high school student.

My love of learning became an additional motivation for mentoring. I rate high on Learning on the Strengths Finder assessment and love to learn. I learned a lot about launching and running a program—and a little about mentoring in the first year or two. Since then, I've learned a little about running programs and *tons* about being a great mentor. I've learned from my mentees, other mentors, and anyone who will talk to me. I love sharing what I've learned, which was my inspiration for writing this book.

Formal corporate mentoring as part of leadership development started gaining traction and became more commonplace in the mid-1990s. That's around the time we began to see more women rising through the corporate ranks. I landed a vice president role at that time. The focus of mentoring was to help employees progress more rapidly through their careers. The emphasis was on the mentee's development.

I discovered I wasn't the only person who learned from my mentees and the mentoring process. Most growth-minded leaders did too. If we positioned mentoring that way, perhaps more women would want to mentor as an integral part of their development plan. We could structure a mentoring relationship with two tracks: mentee growth *and* mentor growth—a win-win.

I've spoken to over one hundred people while writing this book, read a ton, listened to podcasts and interviews, watched videos, and solicited input on LinkedIn. I'll acknowledge "like attracts like" and many of the people in my orbit and network are "like" me in terms of mentoring and other things (I tried to talk to people who aren't "like" me).

My findings didn't surprise me; most repeat mentors said they learned from their mentees. What surprised me was the number of comments saying they (the mentors) had learned *more* from their mentees than their mentees learned from them (I did not follow up with their mentees to confirm that). In most cases, the "learnings" weren't vague "I became a better leader" or "I learned something new"; the learnings were specific things like social media, remote work, crypto or another emerging industry, cultural awareness, or how to present better on Zoom.

The first part of the book focused on mentoring: what it is, best practices, and how it supports other current challenges in the workforce. We then shifted to some mentoring hot topics, including thorny issues like the gender pay gap. We end where we began—the joy of mentoring and mentees.

I thought I knew a bit about mentoring and I'd explored various topics with my mentoring partners. I thought I had a handle on the top mentoring issues for women mentoring women. Not so much. Every conversation gave me something new to think about. How did I miss values when I have my core personal values on a tea-stained index card on my desk where I do most of my writing?

My fellow mentors' support, including many I didn't know, overwhelmed me. They commented on LinkedIn posts and then graciously agreed to speak to me to share their mentoring experiences and insights. I didn't have enough time to talk to everyone who offered to help. Most people are mentoring and exploring different forms and more diverse mentees. As with my mentees, the mentors I spoke to inspired me to do more and write more.

My current mentees are all based in the United States and are mid-career. As a woman who is well past the midpoint in both my life and career, I need to be a little selfish and find mentees earlier in the professions, in different places physically and otherwise, to support my learning.

I hope this book has either provided insight to mentor more or, if you are not yet a mentor, provided the spark to get you started. If you are reading this book, you have more than what it takes to be a mentor, and there are plenty of people looking for *you*!

Whether you are a veteran or a newbie, I hope I've helped answer the question "what will we talk about?" and provided some thoughts on areas you might want to explore with your partner.

So, what do you do next? Here are some thoughts:

- Find or add a mentee—or two or more.
- Diversify your mentoring: different forms, different mentees.
- Think a bit more about how mentoring can help you. Where do you need to develop? Be intentional about working on those development needs in your mentoring planning.
- Consider starting a mentoring program at your organization.
- Find a reverse mentor; you will both benefit.
- Encourage the other leaders in your organization, especially your team, to mentor within the organization and outside.
- Enjoy and learn!

I ask the question "what have I missed?" a lot—about a lot of things. The answers often come at the most unlikely times and in unlikely places. And often, it's when I was walking my dogs; I intentionally don't listen to anything on my phone when we take our short walks.

I was on a midday stroll with my senior (age unknown as he's a rescue, but at least thirteen), lumpy, overly friendly Basset Hound. As Gus lifted his leg, it came to me.

I've never had a formal mentor—it wasn't a "thing" when I started my career, and I was not aware of any mentoring programs. I've certainly had a lot of supporters. I started mentoring and learned the value of mentoring for both partners. I still didn't have a formal mentor now.

More often than not, when I speak to mentors over a certain age, they say the same thing: "I've never had a mentor." It became something between an excuse and a badge of honor. So, I will close with a call to action to you, my reader and dedicated mentor. In addition to mentoring more, find yourself a mentor—even if you have one, find another.

And I will do the same. If you'd like to mentor me, please let me know.

ACKNOWLEDGMENTS

I have been overwhelmed with the love and support I've received from this book. They say, "It takes a village"; I have far more than that—my sincere gratitude to everyone who supported me in any way.

I'll start with the person who sparked the flame of this book less than nine months ago, my friend, fellow Chief member, and writing partner, Sandhya Jain-Patel. Thanks for seeing an opportunity I didn't see and supporting me through the process. I would not have written this book if not for you. Thanks to the third leg of our author stool, Jaime Ellis.

To my book team: Eric Koester and the entire Creator Institute team, and to the team at New Degree Press. In particular to my editor Miko Marsh: You made me a writer! Thanks for your insight and your patience. Thanks to everyone on this team; I am eternally grateful for your support.

To my family, who supports everything I do. My sons, Mike and Brian; daughters-in-law, Anna and Lea; my grandchildren, Donny, Molly, Casey, Sidney, and Rory. My mother, Barbara Renaldo, my six siblings, siblings-in-law, and my nieces and nephews. And a bunch of dogs. I love all of you.

To the people who generously supported my crowdfunding campaign and so much more:

A. J. (Tony and Anna) Danza
Abbie Moore
Adrienne Zeigler
Aine McGrath
Alison James
Alyssa Laplante
Amanda Babb
Amanda Lopez
Amber Webb
Amy Conway-Hatcher
Amy Stuhmer
Amy Horner
Andrea Cahn
Anna and Mike Ferguson
Anna Malhari
Annu Khot
Aparna Sarin
Asha Aravindakshan
Barbara J Bunk
Barbara Renaldo
Beatriz Loizillon
Bernadette Lawler Sciarabba

Betsy Bergeron
Brian and Lea Ferguson
Brian McLaughlin
Callie Reynolds
Carmen Bohoyo
Cathleen Dohrn PhD
Cathy McCabe
Cecilia Patricia Pellicer Blanco
Charisse Sparks
Cheryl Stallings
Christine Nader
Ciara Cronin
Cindy Braddon
Cindy Wahlig
Claudia Augustyniak
Colette Dill-Lerner
Crystal Proenza
Cynthia Steele
Dana Gilland
Daniel Renaldo
Deborah Clark
Deirdre Borrego
Denielle de Wynter

Denise Conroy
Denise Kleppe
Denise Robbins
Diane Gelman
Diane Yetter
Digna Louis
Donna Dwyer
Donna Wallace
Ellen Leikind
Eric Koester
Erica Simms
Erin Lenihan
Esther Kuiters
Eugina Jordan
Evonne Inglesh
Fiz Olajide
Gail Taylor
Gary Henn
Gee Johnson
George Schifano
Glory Edozien
Gus Ferguson
Heather Goldin
Heidi Lorenzen
Helene DeVries
Holly Firestine
Irene Pleasure
Jaime Ellis
Jean Collier
Jen Maher
Jennie Martel
Jennifer Ayers

Jennifer Dimenna
Jennifer Paradise
Jennifer Rowland
Jessica Eckrote
Jim Lefebvre
Jim Slevin
Jinny Uppal
Joanne Hickman
Joanne and Peter Renaldo
John and Amy Montuori
John Renaldo
John Scully
Judith Nicolosi
Judy Moon
Julie Burek
Julie Milroy
Kalpana Yendluri
Karen Fessler Strack
Karen Feuer
Karen Matijak
Karen Simonenko
Kelly Slavitt
Kelly Young
Kim Sacramone
Katrina Yolen
Laura Kierman
Lew Bader
Lina Tonk
Linda Brown
Linda Novosel
Linh Lanh
Lionel Phillips

Lisa Cheney
Lisa Friscia
Lisa Rangel
Lisha Davis
Liz Hogan
Loren Greiff
Loren Rosario-Maldonado
Madeline Tamagni'
Maki Kawaguchi
Mara Maceri
Margaret Golden
Maria P. Jordan
Maria T. Ortiz Spillane
Marion Parrish
Marisol Perez
Marissa Fernandez
Marissa Shapiro
Martin Dahlborg
Mary O'Reilly
Maryellen and Mark Valaitis
MaryJo Thomas
Maura Charles
Megan Bloomer
Melanie Murphy
Melissa Cohen
Melissa Wojtyla
Mia and Lark Renaldo
Michael Colacino
Michelle Bufano
Michelle Faison-Oldham
Michelle Finocchi

Michelle Ng
Michelle Stevenson
Monica Richter
Myriam Fernandez de Heredia
Nafissa Benhassine
Nancy Mattenberger
Nicole Bliss
Nitin S Joshi
Paru Radia
Patricia Romboletti
Paul Henrietta
Peg and Ray Warren
Petra Sansom
Potoula Chresomales
Quyen Tran
Rachel A. Canning
Randi Nolan
Rani Nagpal
Rebecca Blaho
Reema Pinto
Renee Ryan
Robert Donato
Robert Peters
Rosalind Danner
Sandhya Jain-Patel
Sandra Tripp
Sara Wong Hilton
Sarah Bierenbaum
Sasha Purpura
Shubhra Kathuria
Sofia Pertuz

Stephen Renaldo
Steve Debow
Sudeshna Sen
Sue Bolton
Susan Gouijnstook
Susan Heard
Tamara McCarthy
Tara May
Wendy Fisher

Thomas J. Kilkenny
Ting Piper
Tony Steadman
Tricia Dunn Maggio
Trixie Ferguson Gray
Victoria Chu Pao
Walter Heard

To the hundreds of people who provided content for this book through interviews, talks, and participating in my endless polls and posts on LinkedIn, thanks for your time and your insight. Special thanks to my beta readers; my book is better because of your input. In particular to Nicole Smart who read the chapter on DEI.

To my fellow Chief members. You have been with me every step in this process, providing insight, financial support, feedback, and, most importantly, emotional support.

Thanks to my mentees, who not only provided great content and stories for this book but helped me become a better mentor and a better person. Thanks to my former colleagues at S&P Global–McGraw Hill, who fueled and supported my passion for mentoring. That includes my mentoring program co-founders, Rose Lanard and Lin Carvalho. And to Sue Stanek, and Lynn Sontag of Menttium. To all of our Implementation Team members and participants in the programs. Rachel Thomas and Alicia Scaturro did so much of the actual work and always made me look good.

APPENDIX

INTRODUCTION

Hinchcliffe, Emma. "The Female CEOs on This Year's Fortune 500 Just Broke Three Records." *Fortune.* June 2, 2021. https://fortune.com/2021/06/02/female-ceos-fortune-500-2021-women-ceo-list-roz-brewer-walgreens-karen-lynch-cvs-thasunda-brown-duckett-tiaa/.

"Mentoring During COVID." UC Davis Health. Accessed March 2, 2022. https://health.ucdavis.edu/ctsc/area/education/mentoring-academy/covid-19-resources.html.

CHAPTER 1

Gundlapalli, Ravishankar. *The Art of Mentoring.* Scotts Valley: CreateSpace Independent Publishing Platform, 2017.

JAgyasi, Prem. Dr. Prem. https://drprem.com/quotes/self-mentoring-thus-is-advisable-for-individuals-who-love-the-idea-of-growing-nurturing-and-building-their-life-without-any-outside-influence/.

CHAPTER 2

Dweck, Carol S. PhD. *Mindset: The New Psychology of Success.* New York: Ballantine Books, 2007.

CHAPTER 3

"Our Story." Art of Mentoring. Accessed March 2, 2022. https://artofmentoring.net/our-story/.

Covey, Stephen R. *The 7 Habits of Highly Effective People.* New York: Free Press, 2004.

Dweck, Carol S. PhD. Mindset: The New Psychology of Success. New York: Ballantine Books, 2007.

Ofgang, Erik. "PISA Report: A Growth Mindset Can Lead to Better Student Outcomes." Tech & Learning. April 15, 2021. https://www.techlearning.com/news/pisa-report-a-growth-mindset-can-lead-to-better-student-outcomes.

Oxford Learner's Dictionaries. s.v. "mindset." Accessed March 2, 2022. https://www.oxfordlearnersdictionaries.com/definition/english/mindset.

Richardson, Melissa. "Mind Your Mentoring Mindset." The Art of Mentoring. Accessed March 2, 2022. https://artofmentoring.net/mentoring-mindset-2/.

Romboletti, Patricia. *Bulletproof Your Career: Secure Your Financial Future and Do Fulfilling Work on Your Own Terms...for LIFE.* Atlanta: Bulletproof Publishing, 2018.

Yeager, David S., Paul Hanselman, Gregory. M. Walton, Jared S. Murray, Robert Crosnoe, Chandra Muller, Elizabeth Tipton, et al. "A National Experiment Reveals Where a Growth Mindset Improved Achievement." *Nature*. August 7, 2019. https://www.nature.com/articles/s41586-019-1466-y.

Zenger, Jack and Joseph Folkman. "How Age and Gender Affect Self-Improvement." *Harvard Business Review*. January 6, 2016. https://hbr.org/2016/01/how-age-and-gender-affect-self-improvement.

CHAPTER 4

"Women in the Workplace Report." Lean In. Accessed October 1, 2021. https://leanin.org/women-in-the-workplace-report-2021.

CHAPTER 5

Colletta, Jen. "Why COVID-19 Has Made Mentoring for Women a Must." Human Resource Executive. August 11, 2020. https://hrexecutive.com/why-covid-19-has-made-mentoring-for-women-a-must/.

"Seven Charts That Show COVID-19's Impact on Women's Employment." McKinnsey & Company. Accessed October 5, 2021. https://www.mckinsey.com/featured-insights/diversity-and-inclusion/seven-charts-that-show-covid-19s-impact-on-womens-employment.

CHAPTER 6

Austin, Robert D. and Gary P. Pisano. "Neurodiversity as a Competitive Advantage." *Harvard Business Review.* May-June 2017. https://hbr.org/2017/05/neurodiversity-as-a-competitive-advantage.

Brown, Eric M. and Tim Grothaus. "Experiences of Cross-Racial Trust in Mentoring Relationships Between Black Doctoral Counseling Students and White Counselor Educators and Supervisors." *The Journal of Community Psychology.* Accessed March 2, 2022.

https://tpcjournal.nbcc.org/experiences-of-cross-racial-trust-in-mentoring-relationships-between-black-doctoral-counseling-students-and-white-counselor-educators-and-supervisors/.

Brown, Nadia E., and Celeste Montoya, "Intersectional Mentorship: A Model for Empowerment and Transformation." *Cambridge University Press.* October 16, 2020.

https://www.cambridge.org/core/journals/ps-political-science-and-politics/article/abs/intersectional-mentorship-a-model-for-empowerment-and-transformation/6973ED51EF068A3B28C6CEFDF0048833.

Kaufman, Michelle R., Kate Wright, Jeannette Simon, Giselle Edwards, Johannes Thrul, and David L. DuBois. *American Journal of Community Psychology.* July 28, 2021. https://doi.org/10.1002/ajcp.12543.

McKinsey & Company and LeanIn.org. "Women In the Workplace 2020." Lean In. Accessed on October 15, 2021. https://leanin.org/women-in-the-workplace-report-2020/the-state-of-the-pipeline.

Moseley, Rachel L., Tanya Druce, and Julie M. Turner-Cobb. "When My Autism Broke: A Qualitative Study Spotlighting Autistic Voices on Menopause." National Library of Medicine. *PubMed* 24, no. 6 (August 2020): 1423-1437. https://10.1177/1362361319901184.

Oxford Learner's Dictionaries. s.v. "intersectionality." Accessed March 2, 2022. https://www.oxfordlearnersdictionaries.com/us/definition/english/intersectionality.

"Generational Differences in the Workforce [Infographic]." Purdue University Global. Accessed on October 15, 2021. https://www.purdueglobal.edu/education-partnerships/generational-workforce-differences-infographic/.

CHAPTER 7

Flachsenhaar, Matt. "Mentorship Is Extremely Selfish. Do it Immediately." LinkedIn. July 24, 2019. https://www.linkedin.com/pulse/mentorship-extremely-selfish-do-immediately-matt-flachsenhaar-flax-/.

Kondo, Marie. *The Life-Changing Magic of Tidying Up.* New York: Ten Speed Press, 2014.

Ravenscraft, Eric. "Practical Ways to Improve Your Self-Confidence (and Why You Should)." *New York Times.* June 3,

2019. https://www.nytimes.com/2019/06/03/smarter-living/how-to-improve-self-confidence.html.

Robison, Bryan. "5 Tips to Steer Clear of - The 2021 Sharply Rising Burnout Epidemic." *Forbes.* August 28, 2021. https://www.forbes.com/sites/bryanrobinson/2021/08/28/5-tips-to-steer-clear-of-the-2021-sharply-rising-burnout-epidemic/?sh=2b-8f22ac555a.

Say, Rosa. "Selfish Mentoring." Lifehack. Accessed September 15, 2021. https://www.lifehack.org/articles/featured/selfish-mentoring.html.

CHAPTER 8

"Important Networking Statistics Everyone Should Know." Apollotechincal. January 4, 2022. https://www.apollotechnical.com/networking-statistics/.

Marc Kaschke. "Refining the Diamond That Already Exists." October 12, 2021. Video, 26:03. https://www.youtube.com/watch?v=t1GzRenCZO4.

"LinkedIn Learning's Fifth Annual Workplace Learning Report." LinkedIn. Accessed March 2, 2022. https://learning.linkedin.com/content/dam/me/business/en-us/amp/learning-solutions/images/wlr21/pdf/LinkedIn-Learning_Workplace-Learning-Report-2021-EN-1.pdf

Wronski, Laura. "CNBC|Survey Monkey Workforce Happiness Index: April 2021." Accessed March 2, 2022. https://www.

surveymonkey.com/curiosity/cnbc-workforce-survey-april-2021/.

CHAPTER 9

Covey, Stephen R. *The 7 Habits of Highly Effective People.* New York: Free Press, 2004.

Lupu, Iona and Mayra Ruiz-Castro. "Work-Life Balance Is A Cycle, Not an Achievement." *Harvard Business Review.* January 29, 2021. https://hbr.org/2021/01/work-life-balance-is-a-cycle-not-an-achievement.

"Work Life Balance." Mental Health Foundation. Updated September 21, 2021. https://www.mentalhealth.org.uk/a-to-z/w/work-life-balance.

CHAPTER 10

Barroso, Amanda and Anna Brown. "Gender Pay Gap in U.S. Held Steady in 2020." Pew Research Center. May 25, 2021. https://www.pewresearch.org/fact-tank/2021/05/25/gender-pay-gap-facts/.

"Black Women Aren't Paid Fairly." Lean In. Accessed October 1, 2021. https://leanin.org/data-about-the-gender-pay-gap-for-black-women.

Nathwani, Anjana. "The Perfection Trap." LinkedIn. January 21, 2021. https://www.linkedin.com/pulse/perfection-trap-anjana-nathwani-global-goodwill-ambassador/.

"Women in the Workplace Report." Lean In. Accessed October 1, 2021. https://leanin.org/women-in-the-workplace-report-2021.

Made in United States
North Haven, CT
13 May 2022

19139509R00107